EARLY CHILDHOOD EDU

Sharon Ryan, E

ADVISORY BOARD: Celia Genishi, Doris Fromberg, Carrie Lu
Amita Gupta, Beatrice Fennimore, Sue Grieshaber, Jackie Marsh, Mindy Blaise, Gail Yuen, Alice Honig,
Betty Jones, Stephanie Feeney, Stacie G. Goffin, Beth Graue

To look for other titles in this series, visit www.tcpress.com

(continued)

THE NEW
EARLY CHILDHOOD
PROFESSIONAL

A STEP-BY-STEP GUIDE TO
Overcoming
Goliath

Valora Washington
Brenda Gadson
Kathryn L. Amel

FOREWORD BY ROGER AND BONNIE NEUGEBAUER

TEACHERS COLLEGE PRESS
TEACHERS COLLEGE | COLUMBIA UNIVERSITY
NEW YORK AND LONDON

National Association for the
Education of Young Children
Washington DC

Published simultaneously by Teachers College Press, 1234 Amsterdam Avenue, New York, NY 10027 and the National Association for the Education of Young Children, 1313 L Street NW, Suite 500, Washington, DC 20005

Library of Congress Cataloging-in-Publication Data

Washington, Valora, 1953–
    The new early childhood professional : a step-by-step guide to overcoming
        Goliath / Valora Washington, Brenda Gadson, Kathryn Amel.
        pages cm. — (Early childhood education series)
    Includes bibliographical references and index.
    ISBN 978-0-8077-5663-8 (paperback : acid-free paper)
    ISBN 978-0-8077-7384-0 (E-book)
        1. Early childhood education—United States. 2. Early childhood educators—
    United States. 3. Educational change—United States. I. Title.
    LB1139.25.W376   2015
    372.21—dc23   2015008895

ISBN 978-0-8077-5663-8 (paper)
ISBN 978-0-8077-7384-0 (ebook)

NAEYC Item # 1127

Printed on acid-free paper
Manufactured in the United States of America

22   21   20   19   18   17   16   15   8   7   6   5   4   3   2   1

To the

680 CAYL Fellows

with whom we have worked from

2004–2014

Thank you for being part of our beloved confidential community!

Contents

Foreword

It's magic! That's what it feels like when you encounter high quality in an early childhood setting. But quality doesn't magically happen. It is carefully constructed from a host of building blocks—staff who are both knowledgeable and nurturing, environments that feel both safe and stimulating, a curriculum that is child-focused, a respect for parents, effective advocacy for children and families, and so on. One professional checklist of quality provided more than 200 items to consider!

This is not to say, however, that every building block is equally important. When one element of quality is provided in a powerful way, this can more than make up for deficiencies in other elements. For example, in a township in South Africa we were amazed by how the sincerity and exuberance of two teachers brought joy and stimulation to 30 children, even though the environment was dismal—a small room with a dirt floor and no windows.

But one element is unequivocally necessary—leadership. A talented leader is required to pull all the building blocks of quality together into a harmonious community. For this reason, *The New Early Childhood Professional: A Step-by-Step Guide to Overcoming Goliath* is a vital resource for both new and experienced early childhood leaders.

We have been publishers of *Exchange*, a magazine for early childhood leaders, for nearly 4 decades. In that time we have read (or started to read) hundreds of books on leadership. There are the "heroes of industry" books where successful bosses of Fortune 500 companies, such as Donald Trump and Howard Schultz, tell you why they are so great—really useful stuff if you plan to live in the privileged world of multinational titans. Then there are the books of or by theorists like Peter Drucker and Warren Bennis, in which you learn about the science of leadership—these books may be inspiring, but somehow they don't really speak to a director with a budget in the red, an overflowing toilet, and two teachers calling in sick.

That is why *The New Early Childhood Professional: A Step-by-Step Guide to Overcoming Goliath* is so exceptional. It is based not just on one person's story of how organizations work. Rather, in this book Valora Washington, Brenda Gadson, and Kate Amel have constructed an inspiring, yet practical game plan for emerging leaders from the insights and experiences of dozens of practicing early childhood leaders. This is a book based on the realities, the challenges, and the possibilities of the early childhood field.

Indeed, the early childhood field provides many unique challenges for leaders. The work is extremely important. Brain research has validated the belief that the nurturing and stimulation children experience in the early years goes a long way in shaping the trajectory of their life experiences. Yet this critical work is woefully underfunded. An early childhood leader must craft a quality program without being able to pay teachers wages commensurate with the critical work they perform, and with limited resources to construct an ideal environment.

And the pathway to quality is not set in stone. Advocates for quality argue endlessly about the focus of curriculum: Should a program be child-driven, built around play and curiosity? Or should it be teacher-driven, focusing on early academic achievement? At the same time, debates swirl around the qualifications of teachers: Should every teacher have a BA degree, or are other skill and temperament factors more important?

Other curriculum debates abound: Should a program protect its children from every possible risk, or should children be allowed to take risks and learn from the consequences? Should a program immerse children in the latest technology, or is interaction with real materials and real people more important? Should time outdoors be considered as simply a recess, or should connecting children with nature be a central tenet of the program?

An early childhood leader must be able to wend her way deliberately and thoughtfully through the many unique decision points of our field. She must design a pathway to quality that makes sense to her and the community she is serving. She must be prepared to face Goliath with confidence and persistence.

The authors' game plan leads the reader through four stages of preparing to face Goliath:

- **Analyze**—When confronting seemingly insurmountable situations, instead of being overwhelmed, think and reflect about the situation and discover hidden insights.
- **Advance**—Plan and prepare for the pathways to achievement.

- **Act**—Start with everyday challenges; find hands-on applications of real-time problems; provide the footing needed for the bigger challenges ahead.
- **Accelerate**—Focus on what you want to change, gather allies, document, and communicate.

This is not a conventional leadership handbook. Along the way, the authors introduce readers to a wide range of unconventional, yet inspiring concepts. Readers are challenged to become "architects for change" and "disruptive innovators," and to do so with intentional communication, authenticity, and transparency. They are encouraged to be prepared to face "asymmetrical conflict" while learning how change happens and building professional capital.

Readers, be prepared to be jolted out of your comfort zone. This book will challenge, inform, provoke and inspire you. Yet, unlike magic, this is not done solely in the service of entertainment or superficial grandstanding. The authors are equipping you to be a valued architect for change.

—Roger and Bonnie Neugebauer

Acknowledgments

We are grateful to many people whose lives and work have made this book possible.

At the top of the list are the 680 CAYL Fellows with whom we have worked in our first decade, from 2004–2014. While this book shares the stories of about 20 CAYL Fellows, the themes of the book are drawn from the work of all of them. This extraordinary group of people shared with us their aspirations, joys, and hopes along with their frustrations, fears, and concerns over many years. We can never repay them for the gift of their time, and the deep bonds of trust as they shared their wisdom, insights, and expertise with us and with one another. These exceptional people deepened our love for both the early care and education field and for the professionals who do this work.

Next we acknowledge the many funders who have made this work possible over many years. Three foundations are particularly noteworthy: Rosa Smith, Greg Jobin-Leeds, and Lynson Beaulieu of the Schott Foundation for Public Education believed in and invested in this work when it was barely an idea. Kim Haskins of the Barr Foundation encouraged us and created forums through which we could think strategically. And with Pam Perrino, Janet Weisberg, and Jennifer Rollins of the Raymond John Wean Foundation, we developed a great passion for working in the Mahoning Valley of Ohio and embraced their deep devotion to the revitalization of the area.

The CAYL Institute is fortunate to have a Governing Board with a deep commitment to the issues and the professionals profiled in *The New Early Childhood Professional*. Marta Rosa, Jeri Robinson, Doug Baird, and Corrine Corso have shared our journey since 2004, offering moral support and inspiration.

Special thanks are also due to our editors at Teachers College Press. Marie Ellen Larcada heard our many stories over the years, read our first drafts, and graciously transitioned this project to Sarah Biondello when she retired. Sarah moved the project over the finish line!

And, finally, we express our gratitude to the families who have wholly embraced and sustained us over the course of this work. Valora's adult children, Omari and Kamilah, have grown up with the CAYL Institute's mission in their blood and have chosen social justice careers of their own. Brenda's husband, Ollie, as well as her children, Aaron and Danielle, and granddaughter, Kennedi, support the impact of her commitment to the CAYL Institute in the midst of the "retirement" years. And we are thankful for the generous support provided by Kate's partner, Ryan, and her family, Lexi, Carol, and Eric. We realize how lucky we are to have such wonderful family and colleagues.

Facing Goliath
Let's Talk!

Cowardice asks the question—is it safe?
Expediency asks the question—is it politic?
Vanity asks the question—is it popular?
But conscience asks the question—is it right?
And there comes a time when one must take a position that is neither
    safe, nor politic, nor popular;
but one must take it because it is right.
                     —Dr. Martin Luther King, Jr.[1]

This book speaks about *change and change-makers*—early educators asking an essential question of conscience: Are we doing the right thing?

The CAYL Institute (Community Advocates for Young Learners) was established in 2004 to provide a forum for early educators to ask questions, and to seek answers, about our work. A basic CAYL Institute (pronounced "kale") premise is that during this dynamic era of interest in early learning, early educators must be better organized, equipped, and empowered to lead change for both children and themselves.

In the decade since the CAYL Institute's inception, we have engaged in intimate, trusting discussions with hundreds of early educators as they define their dreams, hopes, and fears about change. Representing their voices, this book addresses the questions posed by Dr. Martin Luther King, Jr. from the perspective of early care and education practice:

Is our work popular? Largely due to the successful advocacy of early educators, the public has more interest and more willingness to invest in our work than at any time in history. Once an obscure occupation, early care and education is now a growth industry and a topic of public discourse.

Is our work politic? With public interest comes public scrutiny and new perspectives. Once-novel voices—governors, economists, and school boards, for example—now weigh in and take action about young learners. Our hopes and excitement for change are tempered by concern that the early childhood agenda is moving forward without the full benefit of the experience and expertise that we, as early educators, can bring to the enterprise.

Is our work safe? Many early educators sense the arrival of a new era—gigantic change—for the profession. Many worry that the changes challenge our field's accumulated wisdom, question our practices, and rush too quickly toward academic outcomes. Many of us feel unsafe—intimidated, negated, and isolated—in the face of a tsunami of proposed changes.

Are we doing the right thing? We cannot deny the gap that exists between *what we know* and *what we do* in practice. We have much to offer, and at times the best of our theory, philosophies, and approaches go unheeded or underutilized.

Do we have the courage and support to take a position that may be neither safe, nor politic, nor popular because we know it is right? In order to take a position and stand strong in the face of obstacles to that position, we as professionals need to become a more strongly organized, effective field of practice. We need professionwide leadership!

Are we doing the right thing?! Most children still do not receive high-quality early care and education. Even as millions of dollars have been invested in early childhood systems and infrastructure, the people who work on the front lines earn low compensation and few benefits in spite of rising expectations about their qualifications and the results they will produce. If we acknowledge the realities about what young children need from us, what are our responsibilities to take action? And how exactly do we do so?

Facing Goliath

Many fine analyses of the challenges facing both young children and early educators have shed light on the status of the early education profession. Valora Washington (a coauthor of this volume) and Stacie Goffin struck a chord with their 2007 book, *Ready or Not: Leadership*

Choices in Early Care and Education,[2] by noting two predominant ironies in our field:

> First, the field's knowledge base has exploded in recent years, but this new knowledge has not been implemented consistently and systematically across early care and learning settings. This irony is characterized as a "performance gap;" and
> Second, although the public's understanding about the importance of wisely designed preschool programs continues to grow, early educators face a "credibility gap" when we fail to address poor-quality practice or to insist on the necessary resources to do the job well.

Goffin and Washington encouraged us to act with greater urgency, to better define our purpose and responsibilities in order to counterbalance the prevailing strength of these external influences. But while we educators hear and concur with these calls to action, some of us feel paralyzed. To the individual practitioner, the job ahead might seem too big—too Goliathan—to take the first steps.

In the well-known story of David and Goliath,[3] David's community faced the same emotions: They believed in the righteousness of their cause, but they hesitated to act. Who among us has not felt the quiet despair of feeling weak in the face of the strong?

What Can We Do?

This book speaks about *obstacles to change*—wavering courage, gigantic challenges, and uncertain responses when we feel intimidated, neglected, or isolated. But we know these behemoths, these Goliaths, can be overcome.

It speaks of *the tools of change*—acquired wisdom and knowledge, habits of mind that focus on constructive challenge, and alliances that build us spiritually and professionally, individually and collectively.

For early educators, change is nonnegotiable. The size, force, and direction of change is huge. This book proposes strategies we can use in the face of gigantic odds.

The New Early Childhood Professional recounts some of the heroic stories and strategic approaches used by early educators who participated in the CAYL Fellowship programs between 2004 and 2014. Sensing her peers' thirst for courage and community, Valora Washington established the CAYL Institute to deeply immerse practitioners from different parts of the field, such as elementary schools and family child care, in constructive, active learning that stimulates innovation. The CAYL Institute fosters collegial debate, cooperation, and coordination, typically nudging participants out of their comfort zones to define their own truths and pursue appropriate solutions.

Based on the experiences of CAYL Fellows, this book shares a specific framework—a practical road map—for taking actions to challenge the Goliaths among us. This book offers:

- Four progressive paths with 11 interconnected steps to help every early educator become an architect of change.
- Five smooth stones—resources and tools, just like the stones David carried in his rough cloth bag when he faced Goliath—for each of the interconnected steps.
- An opportunity to reflect after reading each step with questions that will help you apply each step to your own circumstances.

Toward Becoming an Architect of Change

The New Early Childhood Professional suggests a four-path framework with 11 steps toward becoming an architect of change in early care and education (see Figure I.1). Change begins as we *ANALYZE*—think and reflect—about the challenges before us. Then, we—architects of change—*ADVANCE* our cause through planning and preparation, which allows us to understand the asymmetrical nature of our efforts, decide how to face Goliath, and strengthen our collective vision and identity. Now the architects of change are ready to *ACT* with courage and boldness; we align what we know with what we do, beginning with our everyday challenges. Finally, we *ACCELERATE* change by working within a confidential community, focusing on what we want (rather than what we don't want), and communicating impact. Each step in the four-path framework represents a progression that builds on and is interdependent with the others.

The Five Smooth Stones

David brought five smooth stones to the challenge with Goliath. Why five smooth stones? The many stones represent the fact that we must be prepared for whatever faces us: Many ideas, strategies, and people

Figure I.1. Eleven Interconnected Steps Toward Becoming an Architect of Change

Chapter 1: ANALYZE!—Think and Reflect

Step 1: Reality—Face It! We must be honest and contemplative about the challenges and capacities that represent the paths that lie before us.

Step 2: Respect Our Knowledge. We know more than we think we do! We have yet to bring the full power of our knowledge to bear in our work.

Chapter 2: ADVANCE!—Plan and Prepare

Step 3: Recognize Symptoms of Asymmetrical Conflict. We need to recognize the factors of isolation, intimidation, and negation when they occur.

Step 4: Reassess Your Willingness to Face Goliath. Now comes the critical decision: advance or retreat?

Step 5: Revelation—Know Your Vision and Identity. To realize our vision, we must affiliate, belong, and connect to one another and to our profession.

Chapter 3: ACT!—Be Brave and Bold

Step 6: Join a Confidential Community and Share Leadership. As we strive for personal mastery, each of us must share strategies and encourage one another.

Step 7: Begin with Your Everyday Challenges. Think about the issues that you face every day. This is the place where you begin your work.

Step 8: Align What We Know with What We Do. We must use what we know every day, in every situation, in every interaction with a child, parent, peer, or administrator.

Chapter 4: ACCELERATE!—Believe and Achieve

Step 9: Focus on What You Do Want, Not What You Don't Want. Too often we worry away our hours and days thinking about the negative, and focus on what we don't want to happen.

Step 10: Don't Walk Alone—Gather Your Allies. It is simply unwise to walk up to Goliath and face him down without colleagues, friends, and supervisors.

Step 11: Get the Word Out—Document and Communicate Impact. Just as the story of David and Goliath is part of our shared mythology and heritage, our stories as early educators must be recorded for future generations.

are necessary to achieve important goals. If one doesn't work, we do not give up; we have additional ideas in our bags.

Throughout *The New Early Childhood Professional*, we offer resources and tools to use when taking each step, to move forward personally and professionally. We suggest that you keep these five smooth stones in your rough cloth bag as you face your own Goliaths.

Take Time for Reflection

After each step, we offer questions to help you relate that step to your own circumstances. Becoming an architect of change will require a lifetime of investigation. And, as John Dewey taught us, we do not learn from experience—we learn from *reflecting* on our experiences.[4] We would add that active testing of what you are learning is also essential.

One lesson we have learned is that early educators have precious little time to reflect. We encourage you to take time for these reflections, either alone or within your community, to expand both your heart and mind.

Our Hopes

We have four major hopes for this book.

We hope that *The New Early Childhood Professional* **will help you become architects of change, not simply reactors to the change occurring around us.** You can learn how to change the rules of the game rather than be overwhelmed by Goliath-sized obstacles. We can repeatedly stand awestruck at the size of our problems, or we can practice patterns of action that set and sustain a course of change. Each of us has the ability to be exceptional so that every child, regardless of zip code, has a world-class early education.

We hope that because of *The New Early Childhood Professional,* **you will learn and gain insights from the experiences of the early educators who have shared their stories.** These change agents talk about the attitudes, beliefs, behaviors, and strategies they used to address their everyday Goliaths, often without an influx of large sums of money or other resources.

We hope that *The New Early Childhood Professional* **will inspire you to participate in a new vision and shared identity among early educators.** We must reduce our individual and collective sense of isolation—we share similar concerns and capacities. Alone, in the darkness of separation, we might focus on what's wrong, but together we can find the spirit to craft solutions for sustainable change.

We hope that *The New Early Childhood Professional* **will strengthen your resolve and help unite us in making our nation even stronger in the future.** A towering goal, to be sure. Yet we would all agree: Education is the foundation of all other professions. We should be proud of the accomplishments of our public education system and of the astonishing contributions we have made as early educators to our nation's growth. We must champion early care and education practice as a foundational part of America's public education system, even when our programs are not located in a "school." Essential to that conversation: How will we measure what counts in early learning, and not just count what is easy to measure?

Let's Talk

We are glad that you have chosen to spend some time with this book and consider the ideas within to help you and our profession to become stronger, more effective, and more authentically respected and appreciated.

The era of survival is over. The time to thrive has arrived. Let's talk—heart to heart!

THEORIES ABOUT SOCIAL CHANGE

The 11-step framework in *The New Early Childhood Professional* is informed by several theories of social change. Thomas Kuhn's theory of change reminds us that people are unlikely to abandon an ill-functioning paradigm, even in the face of remarkable struggle, unless and until they really can see a better and realistic paradigm.[5] Georg Hegel theorizes that every existing social arrangement or intellectual belief system represents a "thesis," often opposed by an "antithesis." In the struggle between the two, synthesis often emerges as something new and unique—a hope we align with our ideas about asymmetrical conflict.[6] In Dao De Jing's theory, change is slow, congruous, and continual—almost imperceptible. His classic example is that of water slowly but surely wearing away at a stone.[7] We use this metaphor as a reminder that every time we make a change, it may be undetectable to others, but it is part of a larger process that matters. Finally, *The New Early Childhood Professional* considers the new social movement theory, an idea that suggests that the postindustrial economy spawned a new wave of social movements that are distinctive because, through them, people construct their identities and focus heavily on social and cultural concerns.[8] Our vision is that we early educators will transform our professional identities, predominant culture, and ideology, forging a new and commonplace shared identity among us.

ANALYZE!—Think and Reflect
What Would David Do?

When we open our hearts, we may begin to notice situations that we overlooked before. We may notice what appear to be insurmountable situations. We could feel overwhelmed—or we could analyze (think and reflect about) the situation and discover hidden insights.

What did David do when he faced Goliath? When David dared to challenge him, Goliath laughed at the young boy's small size and apparent weakness. At first, David agreed to play by the rules. To conform to tradition, he put on a coat of armor and brass helmet and wielded a heavy sword. But, staggering under their weight, David soon realized that those conventional protections would not work for him and, in fact, could work in Goliath's favor. He couldn't move, never mind walk! David took off the traditional protections and reached for tools he knew and understood: a sling and five smooth stones.

When underdogs realize and accept their limitations and decide to use unconventional strategies, they can, and do, succeed.[1] The prevalence of underdogs is an historical fact, as well as a recurring theme in our new mythologies and popular culture ("Size matters not," teaches the diminutive Yoda in the *Star Wars* saga).

Little guys don't succeed out of chance or luck. David, for example, used four important personal strengths in his approach to Goliath that we early educators can summon in our own efforts to beat the odds. New insights about our most challenging circumstances are possible. Consider:

1. *David had a vision.* He knew exactly what he wanted to achieve, and he felt passionately about it. David's vision enabled him to see past his current realities.
2. *David had a clear sense of his identity and his mission.* He believed in himself, and he was clear about who he was.

3. *David used what he knew from the past to inform his future actions.* As a shepherd, David often protected his flock from animals. The simple awareness that he had used his skills—his assets—to succeed before made it possible for him to see success in his future. What he knew and what he did were in alignment.

4. *David was ready to act with courage.* His peers may have been too paralyzed by the size of the problem to act, but David was focused on solutions.

The First Two Steps

Our first two steps can be difficult because they require us to notice and analyze some painful realities:

Step 1: Reality—Face It! Admit that we face persistent, dominant realities that threaten our ability to serve young children fully and well, our capacity to advance as a profession, and our nation's economic future.

Step 2: Respect Our Knowledge. We recognize that there are multiple truths: We know more than we think we know, we have more knowledge than we put to use in our work—in other words, we know more than we do, and there is much more to learn.

These first two steps are part of the "action before the action"—the analysis that takes place before we create and implement a plan for change. Steps 1 and 2 strengthen our ability to notice: to decide what is important and noteworthy about a situation; to make connections between the situation at hand and the broader principles they represent; and to think through a problem using what we know about it. Therefore, in Chapter 1, we begin our journey as architects of change by noticing the realities all around us and by questioning the gap between knowledge and practice.

ANALYZE!—Think and Reflect

Step 1: Reality—Face It!

What can **you** do now?

As you're reading Step 1, identify and analyze the persistent, dominant realities that threaten our children, our families, early educators, and our nation.

Face reality as it is, not as it was or as you wish it to be.

—Jack Welch, former CEO of General Electric[2]

David's ability to face reality is an ancient wisdom that we now see as a leadership principle of the modern world. In his book *Good to Great*, Jim Collins recognizes that great organizations "confront the brutal facts of the current reality."[3] We cannot change what we do not face.

Philosophies, Priorities, Values, and Sentiments

Powerful historic, social, and ideological forces shape our nation's policies and priorities about young children. Forty years later we continue to face formidable, asymmetrical challenges identified in Gilbert Steiner's 1976 book, *The Children's Cause*,[4] a frank analysis of our historic failure to develop a comprehensive policy for children or to effectively coordinate its many early childhood programs and initiatives.

Certainly we have made progress since 1976. In the face of uneven odds, we Americans are ever confident that change is possible. Like everyone else, early educators are bathed in an ethos of "American exceptionalism," the country's pride of position as "leader of the free world," and the inherent strength in our constitutional system and egalitarian values.

But just as freedom is not "free," change does not occur without effort. Our legacy is strong, but we must face realities so that our future will be strong, too. Each generation's commitment to Horace Mann's philosophy of education as a "great equalizer"[5] is rigorously tested when facing its realities: How do we address the plight of former slaves? Of children with different abilities? Of young learners who speak languages other than English? We test our current

11

circumstances when neither "exceptionalism" as an ethos, nor "equality" as a philosophy, aligns with reality. That's why today, as in generations past, change is a result of what we actually and continually do as leaders for young children and for our profession.

America—leader of the free world? Not when it comes to the care and education of young children. Among our realities: There is an international education achievement gap and insufficient progress in closing it. Other nations invest greater resources to create and sustain *systems* of caring for children under age 5.[6]

Systems matter—but values matter, too. Among the many extraordinary communities in Africa, the Masai, well known for their warrior traditions, express their values with a traditional greeting: "Kasserian Ingera," interpreted as, "And how are the children?"[7]

Great question! Think and reflect: To what extent do our values and sentiments about children represent authentic or symbolic intentions to invest in young children—and the people who care for and educate them?

Persistent and New Realities of Childhood

We acknowledge the persistence of challenges that we face for children, families, and early educators—even as the experience of childhood is transforming before our eyes. Our first step—analysis of our realities—remains critical so that we can ask ourselves *why*, for example, are the problems of poverty, food insecurity, and parental stresses so unrelenting? How do we integrate important, ages-old problems with new, emerging issues?

One new reality that is neither inherently good nor bad: Our children have become "digital natives," comfortable and adept with technology that offers interactive gaming, movies, and unprecedented access to other people, such as grandparents, in faraway places. Both at home and school, children spend more time online and indoors and less time in spontaneous and unstructured opportunities to experiment, invent, and explore.[8]

Diane Thureson, a CAYL Fellow who directs a program that combines typical preschool experiences with a natural science center, worries:

> Some kids just don't know how to play . . . they've had
> something put in front of them or they've been told what to

do from the beginning of the day to the end of the day . . .
our children are getting outside and digging in the dirt, and
experiencing nature, taking trail walks. Yet kids will ask, "When
do we get to watch television, when can I use the computer?"

Jeri Robinson, Vice President of the Boston Children's Museum, adds,

Childhood has changed, but children have not. Kids still need
the essentials: blocks, paint, hands-on play, and dramatic/fantasy
play. The early childhood field has to remain true to who we
are and provide children with authentic experiences; there is no
substitute for this . . . how are we going to get the word out to all
parents?

But parenting has also changed. Some children are kept overly
safe when adults strive to create a life for children with no bumps and
scrapes, no real problems to solve. Hara Marano, former editor-in-chief
of *Psychology Today*, warns about hyperconcerned families and the spec-
ter of "teacup children" who are, ironically, brittle and breakable, not
strong and resilient. Marano speaks of raising a "nation of wimps,"
children incapable of developing socially, emotionally, and neurologi-
cally, and who are overreactive to stress because they have never been
free to climb a tree and scrape a knee—to try, succeed, fail, and discover what makes them happy.[9]
Parents worry that the world just outside their front door can be
dangerous (even as children's homes can be places of potential risk
with violent or sexual content and imagery from television and the
Internet not intended for young eyes). Indeed, children in the United
States have higher rates of victimization compared to both their adult
counterparts in the United States[10] and their child counterparts in other industrialized nations.[11] And we know that exposure to violence
and toxic stress disrupts healthy development and can lead to negative
outcomes later in life.[12]

Poverty: Still Among the Harshest Reality Checks. Poverty gen-
erates considerable toxic stress, and the United States has one of the
highest rates of childhood poverty for all races of children among industrialized countries. About one in five American children was poor
in 2012 and one in ten lived in extreme poverty. Worse, the youngest
children are most at risk for living in poverty.[13]

Early educators notice the toll on young children. As Principal Chrissy Pruitt observes:

> Parents are not with their children as often because they're trying to make ends meet, often working longer hours or several jobs.

Noting the changing economic climate in his town, Principal Scott Taylor notices:

> When I came here 7 years ago, 90% of my kids wore designer clothes and you could tell who came from poverty . . .
> that's changed today with the collapse of the auto and steel industries.

Any child growing up in poverty distresses us. It is especially difficult to face the reality that poverty rates vary dramatically by race, with one in three Black and Hispanic children being poor compared to one in eight White children.[14]

Poverty creates and widens achievement and developmental gaps: 40% of homeless children younger than 6 years old, and 54% of homeless preschoolers, have one or more major developmental delays in language, gross- and/or fine-motor, or social skills, as compared to 16% percent of their housed peers.[15]

Public awareness about these issues is increasing. Even the October 2014 issue of *Reader's Digest* describes the evidence that by age 3, children from economically healthy families have heard 30 million more words than children in poverty.[16]

Also, poverty harms young children's brain development and overall physical health. Food insecurity means that more than one in five children are at risk of hunger and over 16 million children under the age of 18 live in households where they are unable to consistently access enough nutritious food necessary for a healthy life.[17] Dr. Robert (Bob) Walls, recently retired principal in a low-income Ohio community, discovered that many children have very little to eat on weekends or school holidays:

> A kid came up to me, probably the 3rd week of school in my first year as principal, and he says, "Dr. Walls, can I have some food? I am really hungry."

Bob took the child to the cafeteria only to find more children approaching him asking for the same thing:

> I sat down at the table and asked, "Don't you guys eat over the weekend?" They said, "No, we don't have anything to eat." If a kid is hungry, what's he going to think about in class? If his mother has been arrested or someone he knows has died, what will be thinking about? A hungry child or a child in distress cannot be expected to learn at a high level.

Principal Valerie Gumes agrees:

> On many mornings, I'm looking at the kids when they walk through the door to see what's wrong with them physically. Are they prepared to be part of the classroom? If not, I need to call my nurse (who is in another building) or I'm playing nurse.

The Realities of Race, Language, and Ethnicity. Changes in childhood, parenting, and poverty take on new urgency given the substantial demographic shifts in the United States. Since 1980, virtually all types of communities have become more racially, linguistically, and ethnically diverse, although differing in the degree, composition, and pace of change. New immigrants and people of color are redefining cities, replenishing the workforce, and filling our nurseries and classrooms— they now make up a larger share of the population in young age groups.[18] The force of demography itself powerfully indicates that, without a doubt, and more than ever, diversity matters . . . and it matters a great deal. While racism hurts, The National Black Child Development Institute reminds us: "Being Black is not a risk factor."[19]

Our nation, like many others, continues to seek ways to find harmony within this mixture of cultures and languages. Structural inequities abound. A recent study found that public schools spend, on average, $334 more per school year on a White student than a non-White student. Where schools are 90% White, the per-pupil spending disparity was $733 more than those schools with at least 90% non-White enrollment.[20]

Investing fewer resources in some children than in others is unlikely to be a strategy that strengthens our democracy. No longer can some employment sectors, like manufacturing, absorb millions of unskilled workers. And joining the military, once an attractive option for young, unskilled people, is less feasible in today's smaller and more highly technical military.

Today's Realities and Our Children's Futures

What options, then, exist for children who experience poverty or disparities associated with their race or other factors? What can we as early educators do to shepherd children away from this path to undereducation, underemployment, and a permanent residence in the underclass? Many of us worry about these questions, concerned that the political focus is misdirected. "Our children are in need," says CAYL Fellow Angel. "It is a tough environment for them out there." Principal Mary Driscoll laments, "All I hear is, 'How are you going to bring your test scores up?' That's the only conversation from people who make decisions."

For some children, Goliath is getting larger, not smaller. All children face the possibility of living in a society with great disparities. Many early educators watch this wave of young learners bearing down on them and optimistically calculate the chances for a paradigm shift that expands and enriches our practice. Others, tired of the discussion, shrug as the wave approaches, numb with compassion fatigue and frustrated by the dearth of exciting, clear, realistic, and immediate solutions. Some may say, "There will always be the poor . . . it's not a problem that can be solved." What do *you* think? Is there a small mote of truth in that sentiment? Perhaps complete eradication of poverty is not possible—but maybe it *is* possible! David would not allow "impossibilities" to dominate his thinking.

Despite our fatigue, our ebbing and flowing cynicism, our sense of despair about the "where" (will the money and support come from?) and the "how" (will we ever find the strength to mount a campaign that will turn the world around for our impoverished young?), light glimmers ahead.

America seems ready to invest more resources to address these relentless realities. As embraced by the venerable Vulcans of *Star Trek* in their philosophy of IDIC (infinite diversity in infinite combinations), we intend that the arc will bend toward justice as our nation strives to accommodate linguistic minorities in some forms of public assistance and school enrollment.[21] Many resources stand ready to reinforce the cross-cultural competence we will need to meet our early educator professional responsibilities and master emerging societal, developmental, and educational complexities.[22]

When America invests in economically poor children, there is strong evidence that their lives *do* improve.[23] As early educators think and reflect, we see some hopeful realities: We know a great deal more about how to support young children than we did 30 years ago. Of course, we have much more to learn. But a clear belief—a smooth stone to add to our rugged cloth sacks—is that we can play and have played crucial roles in the lives of young girls and boys.

ANALYZE! Think and Reflect

The challenges that we might face when we do our best work for children are Goliathan in scope. Even when children appear stable and healthy, and their environments seem supportive and safe, un-examined opportunities for growth may lie just out of sight. We may give a hungry child a nourishing lunch, but others will be hungry this afternoon. We may extend a hand to a newcomer from another land, but soon we may need that hand to address some administrative red tape. As early educators, we must look up into the blinding sun, meeting Goliath's gaze squarely (even as our knees tremble, our minds desperately scramble for a new strategy, and our hearts hunger for a surge of courage).

Education, it turns out, is not always the "great equalizer" envisioned by Horace Mann: Children who are unprepared tend to remain behind while those who have advantages gain even more advantages over time. Readiness and achievement gaps grow wider during the elementary years.[24]

The story of Ohio education veteran Mary Fran Jones speaks to all of us. When she looked at her realities, Mary Fran was frustrated:

> Every year as I worked with transitioning our children from preschool to kindergarten, we began to see children who we thought were "not ready for school." For a couple of years this was bothersome to me because again my thought process was, "Oh my gosh, these children are not ready for kindergarten." I kept asking "What do we need to do so that we can get these children ready for kindergarten?"

Mary Fran's journey began, but did not end, in frustration, as she became an effective architect of change in her community; she took action (see Step 8).

The passage of time, a better economy, or changing demography cannot guarantee that realities will change. Demographic diversity does not necessarily predetermine any particular outcome. For example, child poverty did *not* improve during the Massachusetts economic boom, and poverty rates only worsened in subsequent years.[25] New leadership strategies must be transformational (within systems and of communities) and focus on issues of opportunity, equity, and justice. These strategies must take into account that the situation is asymmetrical and must address imbalances in power. The odds are not even, they are not in our favor, and they will not improve unless we change. But take heart—after all, we are just at Step 1 in our journey—and remember that facing reality is just that, a first step.

Like David, we survey the realities facing both our child charges and the services we are able to offer them. And the need for competencies—a clear vision, strong identity, well-honed skills, and large doses of courage—are quite evident. David respected his knowledge and skill, giving him the power to activate tremendous potential in service of the people counting on him. Finally, David believed that the moment he put this power to use, the entire world could be transformed for the better.

FIVE SMOOTH STONES

1. *Instincts.* Many of our concerns about the realities around us begin with our gut instincts, our internal GPS system. Many of us use our instincts to make decisions every day—it just comes so naturally that we often don't recognize instincts as a mixture of past experiences, learned knowledge, and current situational cues. Let's pay attention to our guts and listen to the things that are said and not said, done and not done.
2. *Sight.* We see and observe the realities for children and for early educators every day. The realities facing us are pervasive, concerning, persistent—and they will not just go away on their own. More, let's not pretend that we do not see the hungry child, the struggling family, the low-wage early educator. When we see something, say something. If we don't understand something we see, ask questions.
3. *History.* Our collective history informs our current and future realities. Read more about our history in V. Celia Lascarides's and Blythe F. Hinitz's *History of Early Childhood Education.*[26]
4. *Values.* Regardless of one's political views, most of us have been touched in one way or another by the belief that the United States is

"exceptional" in its focus on democracy, liberty, and social progress. While there are many critiques of this point of view, few of us are untouched by values highlighting the possibility of change (not fate), equality (not social hierarchy), and opportunity (not predestination). These values give us hope for positive change in the lives of both children and early educators.

5. *Faith.* Our values lead to faith that tomorrow can be different from—better than—today. As we face our current realities, we do so in full confidence that we can envision and create different outcomes—that we can be architects of change.

REFLECT ON BECOMING AN ARCHITECT OF CHANGE: WHAT WOULD **You** DO?

ANALYZE! Think and Reflect   Step 1: Reality—Face It!

We face our realities before taking action as an architect of change.

1. What are your overall reflections about Step 1?

2. "Face reality as it is, not as you wish it to be," advises Jack Welch. Think and reflect on your own community, alone and with others.

Think and Reflect	Your Analysis	Impact of These Realities
How would you respond to the Masai greeting "Kasserian Ingera": How are the (your) children?		
What disparities or realities are evident for the families you serve?		
What disparities or realities are evident for you as an early educator, compared to other comparable fields of work?		
Do you have any additional concerns?		

ANALYZE!—Think and Reflect

STEP 2: RESPECT OUR KNOWLEDGE

What can **you** do now?

As you read Step 2:

- Reflect on the idea of "tacit knowledge" and the role it plays in our field
- Identify gaps in practice, policy, and public expectations
- Recognize fieldwide challenges to address the gap
- Focus on personal mastery

> In no case is the dislocation between the field—as practiced—and the expertise—as professed—as great as it is in early childhood education.
>
> —Martin Haberman[27]

In the early 1970s, the field of early care and education might have been characterized by the slogan "We believe more than we can prove."[28] Researcher Laura Colker found that most people enter our field with altruistic motivations and a sense of destiny: We wanted to make a mark, a difference, in the world.[29] Principal Cheryl Kirk affirms her calling: "I began my career in early childhood education and that's where my heart has always been." Like Cheryl, Bob Walls' destiny was clear: "I always wanted to be in education, to be a teacher, since the 3rd grade. A teacher inspired me to be a teacher."

Our sense of destiny is heightened as our field moves from being a relatively small—some might say "quaint"—field of work to a much larger, more public enterprise. As the focus on early learners becomes more public, the spotlight moves from "what we believe" to "what we know" and "what we do."

What do we know? Although it's incomplete, we do have a solid base of information about the elements of high-quality early care and education experiences for young children (and quality matters a great deal). We have proven that we can reduce the lifetime achievement gaps between disadvantaged children and their more advantaged peers. We know the value of comprehensive services, family engagement, and collaboration as children transition across settings. And research clearly indicates that highly skilled and well-compensated teachers with specialized knowledge make a difference for child outcomes and program quality.[30]

What do we do? Admittedly, when it comes to how we collectively practice early care and education, *we know more than we do* on a day-to-day basis. Most of us find this situation to be unacceptable. "The idea of having knowledge and not using it for the benefit of children is abhorrent!" declares CAYL Fellow Brenda Powers. In the path to becoming an architect of change, Step 2 requires us to think about the knowledge base we can bring to bear on the realities we discussed in Step 1, or on any early care and education challenge.

Tacit Knowledge Is a Strong Root of Our Practice

The gap between what we know and what we do often begins with the way many of us enter the field. Though specific guidelines have been formulated or put in place (for example: National Association for the Education of Young Children (NAEYC) accreditation standards, the National Child Development Associate Credential™, and statewide Quality Rating and Improvement Systems), the ready-to-hire qualifications of practitioners in early care and education settings vary widely, ranging from a high school diploma to a master's degree. Too often the deciding factors are where you live and your employer's expectations.

Once hired, the "on boarding" experience and opportunities for further development or mentorship depend largely on the employer, although some states are beginning to assume stronger roles.

The passing of knowledge, experience, and history is essential to the growth and health of any profession. Typically, our knowledge base spreads through extensive personal contact and interaction, social networks, and trust: the kind of trust we tend to earn as we work with our colleagues.

It's probable that many of us have acquired many of our skills through tacit knowledge. *Tacit knowledge*—the collection of beliefs, ideas, values, and mental models that shape the way we see the world—can be thought of as "know-how" as opposed to "know what" (facts), "know why" (science), or "know who" (networking).[31] It's the opposite of formal or explicit knowledge—what we may learn in college courses or through formal professional development. At times we are not aware of the knowledge we possess or how to transfer it to others.

We believe that the gap between what we know and what we do is related to the absence of a more comprehensive, formal, consistent, research-based, and fieldwide system of required education and demonstrated competencies. Rather, our practice with young children too often depends on apprenticeships, tacit knowledge, learning "on the job," and the power of our commitments.

Despite many government innovations, opportunities for employed early educators to learn can be limited. Most of us work outside of formal school systems, and therefore our pay and benefits are typically lower, and our staff turnover rates are higher. Rewards and recognition for on-the-job performance are limited. CAYL Fellow Marites MacLean sees this phenomena every day, and expresses concern about the children who experience it:

> Child-care providers certainly aren't getting rich in their jobs. Usually they lack health insurance and don't get paid vacation or sick time. This situation leads to staff turnover, interrupting the familiar care children come to know—the upheaval and loss can be disturbing and interfere with learning. Too often beloved faces disappear without explanation or warning.

We are making strides, but our occupation does not have a strong career ladder, common professional standards, or a professional development advocacy system that builds our capacity and protects our rights. For these and other reasons (see Figure 2.1) some question whether the field of early care and education can be defined as a "profession" at all.[32]

"Shooting from the hip or making things up as they go" is not acceptable to CAYL Fellow Mary Fran Jones. Author Sue Bredekamp warns: "When individuals who are responsible for the care and education of children remain ignorant of the knowledge base, children pay the price. We must continue to learn with and from children, but we must stop learning on children."

So, as Parker Palmer explained:

> Many of us became teachers for reasons of the heart . . . But many of us lose heart as the years of teaching go by.[33]

Scientific Evidence: The Heart of Public Commitment

Tacit knowledge may be a strong root of our practice, but scientific evidence is at the heart of public commitment to our work. The

Figure 2.1. Where Early Educators Stand

Educational Background[1]	Teachers and caregivers in centers: • 39% have at least a bachelor's degree (BA) • 19% have a high school diploma or less • 28% have some college credit but no degree • 17% have an associate degree Listed family child care: • 32% have an associate or bachelor's degree • 34% have some college credit • 34% have a high school diploma or less Unlisted family child care providers: • 47% have completed high school or less
Status and prestige[2]	"The low status afforded ECE (referring to early care and education) work seems to reflect the belief that little separates ECE caregivers from babysitters and families who generally care for children without special training, particularly in settings that are not designed with an educational focus."
Salary	2012 median pay: • Kindergarten and elementary school teachers: $53,090 per year[3] • Preschool teacher: $27,130 per year[4] • Preschool director: $43,950 per year[5] • Family child care: $19,510 per year[6]

1. Snow, 2013; 2. Rhodes & Huston, 2012; 3. U.S. Bureau of Labor Statistics, Kindergarten and school teachers School Teachers, 2014a; 4. U.S. Bureau of Labor Statistics, Preschool teachers, 2014c; 5. U.S. Bureau of Labor Statistics, Preschool and childcare directors, 2014b; 6. U.S. Bureau of Labor Statistics, Preschool teachers, 2014c.

news has spread about the economic, educational, and social impact of high-quality early care and education. Using data from several landmark studies about the positive impact of preschool on success in school and later life,[34] advocates have won the support of Nobel Laureates, economists, educational leaders, federal and state policy-makers, and politicians. National leaders now think of our profession as an industry, one that is important to our neighborhoods, states, and the country. Those who previously had little interest in our work have begun to partner with us to drive the change. Our knowledge base is an engine that boosts our public profile.

Early educators are embracing this new power. We join Parker Palmer in asking: "Is it possible to take heart once more so that we can continue to do what good teachers always do—which is to give heart to our students?"[35] Notice the cascading effects:

- Increasing numbers of early educators are earning credentials and degrees, largely as a result of public policy or employer mandates.[36]
- Projections of the number of early education jobs continue to rise.[37]
- Government and private funders sponsor efforts to energize states to offer early care and education programs.[38]
- Most rewarding, American families are buying into the promise of preschool. Enrollment in early education programs tripled between 1970 and 2010.[39] Despite the fact that in 2013, enrollment in state-funded preschool declined for the first time in a decade, most 3- and 4-year-olds are enrolled in some type of formal preschool experience.[40]
- President Barack Obama became the first president to even mention early childhood in a State of the Union address on February 12, 2013. Citing both the financial and child development benefits of early care and education, he said: "We know this works. . . . Let's give our kids that chance."[41] Obama then reemphasized the importance of investing in quality early childhood education on January 20, 2015, during that State of the Union address.[42]

When we heard these words, our computers and mobile devices pinged incessantly as our colleagues posted joyful Facebook messages and tweeted their approval. But look closely: yes, the President's words did excite us. Yet as they reflect his commitment, they also convey the public's growing expectations—based on the knowledge base—that quality early care and education will bring measureable positive effects.

Uh-oh! What we know and what we do takes on more profound meaning. Suddenly, the secret is out: there is a gulf between promises made and promises realized. The gulf makes the long-standing gap between knowledge and practice concrete—and very, very public. The stakes have gone up. "The conversation has shifted from what early care and education programs can do to the results they produce."[43] Researchers Sharon Lynn Kagan and Kristie Kauerz elaborate:

> In early childhood education, goals and standards shift the starting point of educational pedagogy from the child to the content, shifting a century-old way of thinking about how young children should be educated, and, by extension, how early educators prepare for and carry out their jobs.[44]

A Goliath-sized challenge indeed! The conversation has shifted because when new players buy in, they expect to share influence and power. The shift to greater transparency for early educators gets complicated when accountability is equated with "outcomes," "tests," and didactic practice that many early educators consider to be developmentally inappropriate for young learners. With the public we agree to the investments—but are baffled and disillusioned by the terms of the engagement. Are we ready for change or not?

To some, the pendulum has swung too far: We worry that federal and state leaders are stepping in to define the early care and education agenda without us. In response we now see a spate of books, articles, and advocacy organizations committed to "defending" young children in ways that are informed by both the formal and tacit knowledge comprised by our work.[45]

Closing the Gap Requires Fieldwide Strategies

Winning public support with a knowledge base is further complicated because we know that most early care and education practice hardly resembles the oft-cited landmark studies that have impressed the public. There are at least three major questions that must be addressed in any collective efforts to close the gap between what we know and what we do.

One: What should an early educator know and be able to do? This question reveals the fragility of the early care and education workforce: We lack effective organization to speak for ourselves or for the children and families we serve. Our professional boundaries are ill-defined; we do not have an agreed-upon set of fundamentals that shape job entry regardless of the school or university we attend. Further, despite expressed value for a mixed delivery system, our investments across settings are uneven; and, even as the conversation continues to shift from "what we do" to "what we produce," systems of ensuring ongoing professional development, including the transmission of new knowledge, are haphazard at best.

Two: How do we achieve a stable and appropriate funding platform to support both high-quality programs and appropriate compensation for the people who work in them? Too many family budgets are already stretched by a patchwork of child-care choices. The public purse opens only partially and is not aligned with its expectations for quality care. Ironically, the strength of our knowledge base has raised the public's expectations, almost to the point of expecting us to be miracle workers. We, on the other hand, grateful that *any* public funds are forthcoming, have been timid in articulating what the true cost of quality might be.

Even a cursory look demonstrates wide differences in state early care and education programs in key areas such as service time, staffing qualifications, and funding. Fixes, notes the Alliance for Early Childhood Finance, typically involve the creation of a new initiative; "something with a catchy name, aimed at a specific and generally limited group of children." Consequently:

> Funds are allocated for the initiative and a set of standards, rules, regulations, and monitoring practices is established to ensure accountability. While each new initiative has something to offer, the approach results in a fragmented system that not only fails to adequately serve America's children and families, but makes it extremely difficult to gather comprehensive data or plan and finance an effective ECE system.[46]

Three: Even if we had the resources, do we have the leadership skills to organize ourselves and to move forward? To close the gap, we *must* develop new skills and competencies. At a minimum, fieldwide leadership requires two criteria: (1) an urgent focus on competencies and demonstrated performance (not just degree attainment) and (2) broad representation. To reveal and integrate best practices, those who deal with policy and those who deal with practice must communicate more often and more clearly. Greater respect for the front-line staff is necessary; today, direct service staff members often feel devalued, poorly represented, misrepresented, or not acknowledged at all as a result of social, economic, cultural, or professional separation from "acknowledged" leadership. Our asymmetrical challenges require adaptive leaders who can, and will, lead from any position without respect to title, position, salary or sector.

In the Meantime: Respect Our Knowledge Base, Focus on Personal Mastery

In Step 2, to close the gap, we emphasize the importance of respecting our knowledge base and closing the gap between knowledge and practice. The new political nature of our work overwhelms us, but most of us accept that, to close the gap, we have a lot of learning to do, including honest self-examination of what we believe about children, what outstanding early care and education really looks like, and where our individual knowledge and skills need work. The early educators who keep on saying, "Trust me, I know how," will not prevail. They must also be capable of saying, "I know why, I know what, and I know who." The rules have changed forever; the "cheese" has already been moved.[47]

The action we take in Step 2 is about adaptation, seeking progressively deeper levels of personal mastery. The CAYL Institute invites early educators to join in communities with diverse leaders, come with questions drawn largely from our everyday challenges, and dive into our knowledge base for direction. While most CAYL Fellows have worked in early care and education for 5 or more years, not many have had structured opportunities to reflect on their work. The first day of a CAYL Fellowship starts hard and fast. Fellows build strength and shape a philosophical framework that will undergird their way of life for years to come. CAYL Fellows are eager to master new ways that they can influence policies and sustain practices that will come into play every workday of their careers.

Typically, Fellows respond to the CAYL Institute's invitation with excitement and engagement: Carrie Boyer says, "I find the knowledge base to be inspiring because it represents the best way to do things. Delving into the knowledge base is becoming a matter of routine for us." Scott Taylor saw in himself "determination to implement these best practices as fast as we can." Bob Walls agreed, saying: "The biggest thing a principal can do is stay on top of what's happening in the education field. The more education and professional development we get as teachers and administrators, the more our kids are going to learn."

As our mastery blooms and we have more strength to close the gap between what we know and what we do, our self-respect grows. There will always be a parent, elected official, taxpayer, convenience store cashier, or Internet blogger who will never stop believing that an early educator is a babysitter for little kids who sleep and eat most of the day, and when the kids are awake, the caregiver might sing the A-B-C song once or twice or 20 times. What could be easier, and why should we pay that person any more than a 14-year-old babysitter for some shopping money?

Uninformed assumptions have real-life implications: If an early educator doesn't need many skills to reach young children, then we might as well assign an underperforming 5th-grade teacher to the younger children. That's when our personal and collective mastery steps up and steps in, upending this flawed logic and delivering on the promise and power of our knowledge base.

FIVE SMOOTH STONES

1. *Doubt.* Not knowing is always the very first step on the way to knowing. Ask ourselves: What don't we know? How can we do better?
2. *Colleagues.* Let's surround ourselves with colleagues who share our commitment to personal mastery. Never overlook the value of trusted colleagues and the power of our combined efforts.
3. *Organizations.* A wonderful resource in our cloth sack is the wealth of organizations that support children and families. Here are several organizations that should be on every early educator's short list of go-to resources:
   - Professional news and trends: National Association for the Education of Young Children, naeyc.org; or National Institute for Early Education Research, nieer.org
   - To start your career: CDA Council for Professional Recognition, www.cdacouncil.org
   - Child-care resources: Child Care Aware, childcareaware.org
   - Infants/toddlers: Zero to Three, www.zerotothree.org; The First 2000 Days, first2000days.org
   - Diversity: the National Black Child Development Institute, www.nbcdi.org; the National Latino Children's Institute, www.nlci.org; NAEYC Position statements on linguistic and cultural diversity, www.naeyc.org/positionstatements/linguistic

4. *Research.* Use the above organizations to keep current on the latest reports and trends. Knowledge is power.
5. *Voice.* Audre Lorde said, "We've been taught that silence would save us, but it won't."[48] Our voices are powerful. Use them to ask questions and to speak up in ways that address the gap between practice and knowledge.

REFLECT ON BECOMING AN ARCHITECT OF CHANGE
WHAT WOULD **You** DO?

ANALYZE! Think and Reflect   Step 2: Respect Our Knowledge

David used the knowledge and skills he already had to unlock the potential within his community.

1. What do you already know? How did you learn it? What role did "tacit knowledge" play in your professional development?

2. Think and reflect on the gaps between knowledge and practice, policy, and public expectations in our field.

Think and Reflect: What Gaps Do You See in . . .	An Example You Know About	What Might Early Educators Do About This Situation?
Knowledge and practice?		
Knowledge and public policy?		
Knowledge and public expectations?		
Anything else?		

3. *What don't you know?* Not one of us has a complete knowledge of the early care and education field. What are some of the most critical gaps in your knowledge base? Identify one or two key questions of interest and track down the relevant information. Of

course, you can begin with an online search, but don't forget that the men and women with whom you work can be wellsprings of information and experience—they may have just the knowledge you're looking for. When you've answered your question to your satisfaction, ask another one. Professional educators are perennial learners.

WHERE WE ARE SO FAR

Chapter 1 of *The New Early Childhood Professional* has covered the first two steps to becoming an architect of change. Step 1 encourages us to think about and reflect on our realities, and Step 2 requires us to question the gap between knowledge and practice while strengthening our personal mastery.

In the next chapter, we will explore how being an architect of change relies on a strategic engagement process that focuses on clearer vision, identity, alignment of knowing with doing, and a willingness to act on behalf of young learners and early educators.

CHAPTER TWO

ADVANCE!—Plan and Prepare
What Would David Do?

As we think and reflect on our realities, many of us become very anxious to "do something." But steady, now—we're still in the formulation stage. Like David, we must plan and prepare before we act.

In Chapter 2, we continue to advise that we take more time for planning and preparing before acting. Taking time to plan and prepare is not the same thing as "doing nothing." As we Advance, we begin to act, think, and communicate like the architects of change we intend to be. Before advancing, we carefully carve out the pathways for what we want to achieve. Indeed, planning helps us to develop the necessary skills and leadership presence we will need when it is time to face Goliath.

Chapter 2 presents three giant steps as we move closer to taking on Goliath. We are wise when we anticipate asymmetrical conflict and acknowledge that, when power is imbalanced, we may sometimes feel intimidated, negated, or isolated (Step 3). Considering the odds, we pause to consider how to enter the situation (Step 4). Finally, we complete the planning and preparation process by being clear about our vision and identity (Step 5).

Though David's story differs from ours, many of the preparation challenges and obstacles he had to overcome are similar to that of the modern-day early educator. Let's explore four similarities.

David lacked critical experience: "You are only a young man," he was told, and Goliath "has been a warrior from his youth." As early educators, often we have little experience in broader leadership or political skills, tools that will equip us to persevere and strive for change against better equipped, skilled, and politically savvy antagonists.

To some observers, David lacked essential skills: he was a shepherd, not a soldier. To some observers, we lack essential skills. We are educators, not economists or psychometricians. Yet we must learn to answer questions about the "return on investment" and "outcomes" that can be expected from our work when it is high quality.

David was criticized and discouraged from moving forward. His older brother, Eliab, chastised and negated him, asking, "Why have you come down here?" We, too, are often belittled and underestimated as people who are "just watching babies."

David had to seek permission from his elders. When he began to speak of his plans to approach Goliath, he was reported to King Saul, who sent for him. As early educators, we often seek validation from others who make legislative or administrative decisions about our work.

Despite these four challenges to his planning and preparation, David nevertheless faced Goliath. He refused to be intimidated, negated, or isolated. He Advanced! And we can too.

Let's move ahead as we plan and prepare to Advance the status of children and of our profession.

THEORY ABOUT EGO DEVELOPMENT

As with David, it is our strong sense of self and identity that will guide and support us as we continue this journey. Ego identity, one of the main elements of Erik Erikson's Theory of Psychosocial Development, is described as the constantly changing conscious sense of self that we develop through new experiences and information. Each chapter in *The New Early Childhood Professional* begins by asking, "What would David do?" We end each chapter by asking, "What would *you* do?" We aspire that you, as an early educator, will have a strong identity and sense of self that enables you not only to meet the seemingly insurmountable challenges you face but to establish and successfully implement your vision.[1]

STEP 3: RECOGNIZE SYMPTOMS OF ASYMMETRICAL CONFLICT

What can **you** do now?

As you're reading Step 3, identify experiences of intimidation, negation, or isolation when you sense it is happening to you, your colleagues, or our field of work.

> I am an invisible man. No, I am not a spook like those who haunted Edgar Allen Poe: Nor am I one of your Hollywood movie ectoplasms. I am a man of substance, of flesh and bone, fiber and liquids—and I might even be said to possess a mind. I am invisible, simply because people refuse to see me.
>
> —Ralph Ellison[2]

To what extent are early educators akin to the invisible man—not truly seen or appreciated for who we are? Do people refuse to see the low pay? The meager benefits? Ours is a situation of invisibility, inequity, and asymmetrical challenges.

Asymmetrical conflict is a term that typically describes a military situation in groups that have unequal power or capacity for action. We are adapting the term asymmetrical conflict in this book to describe the relative inequalities and disadvantages faced by the early educator and faced in the status of children in our society. The exercise of power over us is often experienced indirectly as well as through clear and imbalanced distributions of material resources.

The ancient Chinese strategist Sun Tzu advises that when an enemy "is strong, avoid them."[3] Avoidance in our case is hardly possible: The social and economic position of children—and early educators—must be addressed. We must face Goliath. Establishing equity and equilibrium is a challenge for us—a challenge that is likely to require tactics and strategies that are unfamiliar, unconventional, and uncomfortable for us.

In Step 3 we recognize the impact of asymmetrical power: intimidation, negation, and isolation.

First, Goliath Intimidates

Goliath's first acts were not physical but came from an attitude: intimidation. Standing 10 feet tall, Goliath projected an image of strength and the illusion of invincibility. He challenged by using strong words twice a day for 40 days.

Intimidation can be subconscious or intentional behavior, a tactical strategy: a glowering countenance, impeding or blocking progress, or using abusive or insulting words. Let's look at each of these strategies more closely.

The Glowering Countenance

We want to comply with the official's stern visage that says "Do not cross me; do what I say." But early educators sometimes find compliance difficult because of the complex, sometimes conflicting, array of administrative and funding streams that have no uniform goals, standards, or structures that address staffing or operational conditions and procedures.[4]

The glowering countenance is experienced strongly by both families who apply for child-care subsidies and the providers who accept these subsidies. Our nation's deficit model of child-care support contrasts sharply with countries that rank high in global studies of quality in early education[5] (see Figure 3.1). As illustrated by the findings of

Figure 3.1. Qualities of Nations with High-Ranking Early Care and Education Programs

Nations that rank high in early care and education have several system elements in place that the United States does not have:

- Legal right to early education
- Universal enrollment
- Subsidies
- High bar for early educators
- Well-defined curricula
- Livable wages
- Health, safety, and nutrition standards
- Parental engagement
- Low teacher-to-child ratios

Source: Economist Intelligence Unit, 2012.

subsidy studies in Missouri[6] and Massachusetts,[7] the system is unduly complex, user-unfriendly, and difficult. "The funding seems unstable," says CAYL Fellow Vicki Silberstein, and "requirements for applying are arduous," says Carrie Boyer.

Early educators, directors, and principals know that better coordination would lessen the glowering countenance–but collaboration "is very hard when there is no incentive," says Pam Perrino, a foundation executive in rural Ohio. Moving forward, Pam suggests the application of an important single principle: "We need to put the child at the center of what we do."

Impeding or Blocking Progress

Many educators tell us that they feel blocked, impeded, or bullied when they attempt to put the child at the center. Speaking up about inappropriate instructional or testing practices feels risky in circumstances where the educator is required to implement a downward extension of traditional schooling into the early years. A common reflection we hear is: "Now we have kindergartens that look like 1st grade!" As weak actors we often worry that our work has become focused on turning out large numbers of "products"—namely, numbers showing evidence of measurable achievement.

While we often focus on external blockages, sometimes we ourselves can impede progress if we internalize Goliath by blaming children and families when they do not meet our expectations. Thinking about the toughest realities facing her, Carrie Boyer shared, "It's not really the children—it's the kindergarten staff. They need to adapt and stop saying, 'The preschoolers are not ready.' We need to be ready for them, not the other way around." Boyer admits that some of her staff members have a hard time accepting that idea. "I have had some really candid conversations with a couple of staff members and told them, 'You need to stop. This is the reality. The children are here. We need to figure out what we're going to do with them.'"

Power that impedes or blocks our work might be challenged with two currently unconventional strategies: First, increased professional strength among early educators might lead to more significant levels of self-regulation, autonomy, or power to either police or protect our own members, our areas of expertise, or our interests. As architects of change we would be—we could be—guardians of the knowledge base about early learning as it is being implemented.

A second unconventional strategy in the face of asymmetrical conflict would be a focus on child development, rather than our current deficit approach to family support. Eminent educator James Comer asserts that the absence of a focus on child development from K–12 education probably contributes more to underperforming schools and racial disparities than anything else.[8]

Embarrassed and Frustrated by Pressures to Articulate and Defend Developmentally Appropriate Practice. Some of us have found ourselves in tight spots when a policymaker, administrator, or parent looks to us for the reasons why we have designed our programs in ways that incorporate play and the construction of knowledge. Indeed we have great empathy for families too often caught in a difficult vise: Families feel anxiety to choose the most affordable programs centered on academic school readiness and alignment with Common Core standards as the raison d'être for early childhood programs. At a recent meeting of corporate leaders, two moms of 1-year-olds pulled Valora Washington and an NAEYC staffer aside to express their frustration in seeking child care:

> The programs were so awful. The NAEYC programs were better. But, you don't understand. It's so competitive out there! Our kids have to be ready! When we visit programs we don't see what results they are achieving!

Some policymakers join parents in expressing these concerns. Valora Washington witnessed an intimidating moment in a gathering of 100 early educators speaking with a high-level state administrator and several well-known national experts. During the intimate and collegial atmosphere of the colloquium, the state education commissioner spoke eloquently and passionately about why he did not think developmentally appropriate practice was a "rigorous enough" method of helping underserved children learn in schools. The room fell to a hush. No one had anticipated his direct challenge.

Like the commissioner, many people in the general public are also not convinced. At a social gathering Valora Washington attended, an auto dealer was attributing the exceptional growth of his business to the skill and training of his service crew. Later, he was amazed to hear her talk about the Child Development Associate™ credential. "You actually can get a credential to do *that*?" he asked. "Well," Valora replied, "don't you want the people who work with your child to be as expert as the people who work on your car?" He admitted, "I never thought about it that way." Exactly!

To address these concerns requires our personal mastery of our knowledge base (Step 2). Too often:

- We find it difficult to answer core questions about the distinctive philosophical and practical underpinnings of our early childhood knowledge base.
- We have difficulty communicating about the balance, or false dichotomy, between the play versus academic approaches to the early years.
- We misappropriate the concept of play in ways that defeat the potential rigor and intentionality of high-quality, developmentally appropriate practice.
- We fail to connect our daily work to the powerful lifetime impact we can have on our young charges.

Feeling Disrespected—Bullied—About the Work We Do. Too many early educators feel painfully belittled. How many times have we heard a colleague say, "I just work in child care," when asked about her or his life's work? What a withering self-reflection! In one CAYL Institute study, focus group participants revealed deep cynicism and concern: "The early childhood workforce is so demoralized . . . they don't view themselves as professionals but as babysitters," and "In this field, people feel undervalued, underappreciated, unsupported, and unrecognized" were representative comments.

A sense of powerlessness was felt quite strongly in the early years of the CAYL Institute's leadership programs. As Fellows worked with excitement to create and communicate policy options, they often anticipated rejection from the system: "They will never listen to us," one Fellow lamented. "Who are we to try to tell them what is best?" asked another. Consciously or unconsciously, these Fellows devalued their lived wisdom. However, with time, the CAYL Institute's leaders began to feel some traction with the system. The fact of success and change over time became a motivating reason why people applied for the CAYL Fellowship: "I want to learn to do that, too," seemed to be the shared enthusiasm.

Second, Goliath Isolates

Goliath challenged the troops: "Why bother using your whole army? Pick your best man and pit him against me. If he succeeds, we will all become your slaves. If I succeed, you'll become our slaves and serve us. Give me a good man." It was a typical ploy to call up an image of a person standing alone, disconnected from the others.

While "bowling alone" and "standing alone"[9] may be defining characteristics of the modern world, among early educators there is certainly a sense of feeling vaguely, and sometimes clearly, set apart or cut off from other educators—physically, professionally, and socially. Parker Palmer wrote:

> I call the pain that permeates education "the pain of disconnection." Everywhere I go, I meet faculty who feel disconnected from their colleagues, from their students, and from their own hearts. Most of us go into teaching not for fame or fortune, but because of a passion to connect . . . we want to work in community with colleagues who share our values and our vocation.[10]

Physical Isolation. Many early educators feel physically isolated from their peers. A study of licensed family child-care providers reported moderate to high emotional exhaustion, a feeling of loneliness, and a desire for more contact with other educators.[11] Reported one Massachusetts Head Start educator:

> I work for a preschool program in a public school. There is a clear lack of respect for the preschool teachers. You would think we are all educators and we all work in the same building, but you find that we are talked down to and given tasks that seem remedial.[12]

We hear stories of public school kindergarten or preschool classrooms placed in a remote corner or basement of the building. These early educators are virtually invisible to other teachers in the building and frequently excluded from all-school events. The sense of detachment is exacerbated by unaligned schedules, making it difficult to meet for discussions of curriculum across age/grade levels for the benefit of all children. Before his transformation, Principal Jeff Wolff admits:

I had kindergarten at one end of my building and I had preschool at another end. Preschool parents used to have to park in a parking lot far away and walk their children to the door. Last year we decided to move the Kindergarten classes down with the preschool, so now Kindergarten and preschool are in the same area. They now have a professional learning community together.

Teachers are not the only early educators who feel isolated. Many CAYL Institute center directors and principals speak of pressure to focus on attendance records, test scores, meal counting, and school-district educator evaluation—tasks that tether them to their computers and take away time for connections with teachers and children.

Early childhood higher education faculty members, more than other faculty, report feeling isolation because many of them are adjunct faculty members, hired from semester to semester, without a presence or voice in college governance or program policies.[13] Some suggest that this isolation makes them an "endangered species," and comes from a devaluation of the early childhood degree by some school administrators who want more flexibility in placing teachers when a vacancy occurs.

Professional Isolation. Once when talking with school superintendents about child care, a member of the group stopped Valora Washington in midsentence: "Why do you keep calling them teachers?" he asked with a sneer. "They're not really teachers."

As a school principal, Scott Taylor reports: "I hear comments like, 'It's cute . . . aren't the kids cute? Isn't hanging the snowflake in the classroom cute?'" Scott realizes that the teachers are doing serious work, and to make it less demeans the people who do the work. "People still say to me, 'You have the best principal job in the district,'" Scott said, assuming that his work is less rigorous. "In fact, our high school principal tells me that and I always say to him, 'Let's switch jobs.' He thinks my day is so easy." Scott said that his superintendent spent a day in his building recently and at the end of the day said, "I have a greater appreciation for what you do. On a daily basis, it's amazing." Scott suggested that the superintendent invite some school board members to visit for a day as well. "They need to see it isn't just fluff. It's not just cutting out the snowflake. We have such a critical job."

Many men in the early care and education field, especially those who provide direct services to children, experience professional isolation because of the perception that child development is "women's work," with low pay and closed doors for men who teach. Men, about 3% of the early childhood teaching workforce,[14] are too often stereotyped as sexual predators if they want to work with the very young. Some men feel pressured to leave the classroom and go into administration.[15] In community interviews Patty found several people who bluntly stated, "Men have no business in the early education field."

A form of professional isolation felt by both men and women is the lack of opportunities to be mentored. As the field grows, the need for wise, senior, seasoned practitioner leadership grows. "Elders" are needed to share their experience and knowledge as well as to demonstrate their lived wisdom and core knowledge of our field.

Social Isolation. Low wages and few or no benefits plague the early care and education field, and relief is not in sight. Even among those with college degrees, wages fail to keep pace with those of college-educated women in similar fields.[16]

At the same time, early educators feel the pressure to do more in terms of professional development, degree attainment, and demonstrated child outcomes without a parallel promise for better compensation or better work conditions when they meet those goals.[17]

Indeed, many early educators are themselves eligible for public assistance or work second jobs to make ends meet.[18] Money is seldom a major motivator for early educators, yet the absence of equal pay in the face of higher expectations begs the question, *Does anybody care?* (see Figure 3.2).

Figure 3.2. Negated by Poor Compensation: Comments by CAYL Fellows

"To get quality care you need quality teachers. To keep quality teachers you have to be able to attract them, retain them, and pay them competitively."

"It's a challenging job that pays so little. I teach early childhood educators and I know that living on a wage from a child-care center is nearly impossible."

"It's a vicious circle. There's a revolving door of staff and quality staff that we cannot afford to keep without raising tuition and losing students to cheaper schools."

Third, Goliath Negates

Goliath worked to negate David with harsh words. As he took notice of David approaching with his shepherd's staff, he sneered and asked, "Am I a dog that you come after me with a stick?"

Just as Goliath wanted to negate David's expertise with the sling-shot, often the expertise of early educators is denied, contradicted, minimized, or rendered ineffective. Too often, it is assumed that "any-one" can teach young children, and the early care and education set-tings are a place where problem staff members might do less damage. Overhearing two principals talking about an ineffective 5th-grade teacher, Valora Washington sighed when she heard their solution: "Let's move her to kindergarten."

Negation is often subtle. Alicia Chin-Gibbons says that she and her colleagues "feel disenfranchised every time the school district fails to mention that we are a preschool through high school district . . . and professional development offerings exclude preschool. It feels like a lack of acknowledgment and respect." Concurring, Vicki Silberstein notes instances that when curriculum is being selected and she asks, "Is there a preschool component?" the answer is, "Oh well, we have to check that out."

One group of CAYL Fellows faced a clear example of negation when the Massachusetts Department of Early Education and Care was first established following many years of advocacy. In contrast to the state's population diversity, the founding board was composed of all-White members. In a meeting with the state commissioner (who was not a member of the field), a group of Fellows raised this issue along with ideas about including diversity content in the state's training. The commissioner sharply rebuked the group, stating that there was no reason why an all-White board should be considered problematic. To the commissioner, the ideas suggested were impossible to hear or see.

The hot-button topic of assessing young children—specifically standardized testing—continues to be an area where early educators feel negated, and opportunities for asymmetrical conflict abound. A common refrain is that "We're spending too much time and scarce resources overtesting kids. The kids are bleary-eyed and traumatized and it's not helping them . . . my teachers have weeks spending all the time administering 1:1 tests to children and no time teaching and learning with them." Noting tension between the process focus of ear-ly educators and the product focus of traditional schools, one early educator noted:

[Early educators] are concerned with children learning how
to use a scissor while [the traditional] school-based educators
are more concerned with what a student is making with that
scissor.[19]

One group of CAYL Fellows discussed what they called "naming
and shaming," the practice in their school districts that requires the
public posting of charts showing the names of teachers alongside the
test scores of children in their classes. The Fellows expressed feeling
"slapped across the face," as this practice negated both respect and
relationships in their learning communities.

Many educators sense that large corporations drive the push for
increased testing because they stand to profit handsomely from it.
Among the complaints was that Pearson, Inc. had included corporate
logos and promotional material in Common Core (a relatively "new"
asymmetrical conflict) reading passages.[20]

There are enduring, persistent concerns that voices of color are
silenced, that efforts to diversify the pool of educators are stagnant,[21]
and that most of us have not become sufficiently culturally competent.

Principal Carrie Boyer wondered if some of her staff members
were giving up on teaching children who didn't understand English
very well. Was the staff writing the children off as hopeless? Not worth
putting effort into? Just "extra work"? Whatever they were thinking,
Carrie knew that "We need to figure out what to do for them, come
up with a plan, and provide interventions."

To better understand this dynamic, the CAYL Institute held focus
groups with Latino, Asian, and Black early educators in Massachusetts
to explore perceptions of how leadership for young children is shared
across ethnic groups (see Figure 3.3). Asian, Black, and Latino leaders
expressed experiencing "a sense of professional isolation and margin-
alization." Virtually every individual recalled being the only person of
color at key program or policy meetings, and many spoke about the
pressures they feel to be the spokesperson for their entire group. Their
negation emerged from a number of factors:

- Their ideas and contributions were ignored, often to be
  embraced later when voiced by a White person.
- There is a lack of data about their children and communities.
  Should Haitian and Cape Verdean immigrants be counted as
  African Americans? Are all Spanish speakers appropriately

Figure 3.3 Do You See Us? Voices of People of Color

"There is a real lack of access for upward mobility."

"The field of early childhood education has been conceptualized and led by White women. Deep issues of research, practice, teacher preparation, and leadership need to be addressed to create a public debate that engages all of us."

One person described her colleagues' frustration at a state policy meeting: "They had to fight to say one or two things . . . it feels like they are hitting their heads against a brick wall."

"The onus isn't on us to change them, but they need to hear our voices."

"The current early childhood leadership has been in control for decades, and they are not ready to step aside and share that power. There is a reluctance to share those tables, and those tables don't cater to how we participate."

"Indigenous leadership [is] necessary for sustainability."

From CAYL Institute (2010–2014), *Conversations with Early Educators.*

grouped as Latino despite diverse cultural origins? Does the designation "Asian" properly represent children from China, Japan, and India? By not tracking data by race and ethnicity, one participant said, "It's an excuse to do nothing."

- There are strong perceptions that their collective voice is excluded. Participants pointed out that women of color are concentrated in classroom or support roles and lack the flexibility in their schedules to attend professional meetings or policy discussions that occur during the workday.
- Some people prefer to focus on issues internal to their own communities. Many of these communities have relied heavily on developing their own structures and institutions. Participants spoke passionately about the strength and validation they find within community-based leadership and professional development circles.

We should point out that some of these candid reflections stunned some of the White participants, who acknowledged they had "no idea" that their colleagues had such strong feelings. Although one person dismissed the overall tone as "whining," most listened and learned. One woman said she recognized the value of "hearing it, although it was so striking and painful."

THEORY ABOUT ASYMMETRICAL CONFLICT

The New Early Childhood Professional recognizes the status of children and early educators as weak, relative to both other educators and other professions. Therefore, the work we must do to achieve a stronger position for our children and ourselves is asymmetrical—the odds are not even.

The history and theory of asymmetric conflict are summarized by Andrew J. R. Mack's 1975 article "Why Big Nations Lose Small Wars"[22] and Ivan Arreguin-Toft's *How the Weak Win Wars: A Theory of Asymmetric Conflict.*"[23] Mack and Arreguin-Toft refer to "asymmetric conflict" as a significant disparity in power between opposing actors in a conflict. Arreguin-Toft's analysis specifically theorizes that underdogs can and do succeed when they realize and accept their limitations and decide to use unconventional strategies.

FIVE SMOOTH STONES

1. *Balance.* Inherent in asymmetrical challenge is the effort to keep us off-balance. Stay strong! Realize that we can maintain balance in the midst of attempts to intimidate, isolate, or negate us. Start by acknowledging what's out of balance. Plant our feet on solid ground—on our NAEYC ethical principles—so that we do not teeter-totter. Be precise about how any policy or system is using power so that we can face those Goliaths with clarity and focus.
2. *Affirmations.* Even as others intimidate, isolate, or negate, we affirm. As sharp as negating words can be, they can be dulled by affirmations just as easily as a whetting stone can sharpen. Identify and stay in touch with what we truly want to achieve, or to be. Affirmations create feelings that energize us to action, help us use our energy constructively, and suggest pathways for change. Never make the mistake of returning in kind any hurtful words or phrases that may be directed toward us.
3. *Wellness.* When we're on airplanes, we hear the flight attendant instruct us about how to behave in an emergency: Put on your own oxygen mask before helping other people. This principle can be applied to the whole of life, even when our mission in life is to make life better for other people. It is easy to neglect ourselves. Let's take care of ourselves with the same standard of care that we use with

the people who depend on us. Holding tight to the stone of wellness in our cloth sack is not selfish but rather a loving act for ourselves as well as for those who love us.

4. *Community.* Facing powerful asymmetrical challenges is always difficult, but it is a burden best shared in a community with other people who expand our circle of influence. CAYL cannot state it often enough: Never walk alone!

5. *Invitation.* Many asymmetrical challenges occur because we are not "at the table" when issues are discussed and decisions are made. We have a solution for that: Invite ourselves! This is easier to do than we probably think. Many public bodies have "sunshine laws" that require public input. Don't give in to isolation. Our presence will lead to more invitations. Change is on the horizon.

REFLECT ON BECOMING AN ARCHITECT OF CHANGE
WHAT WOULD **You** DO?

ADVANCE! Plan and Prepare   Step 3: Recognize Symptoms of Asymmetrical Conflict

Early educators often have less power and positional authority when conflicts arise over standards, practices, and qualification requisites. Think about your immediate circumstances and recognize the significant imbalances that you might experience.

1. What are your reflections about Step 3?

2. Are there places or situations where you feel intimidated in your life as an early educator? Where you feel isolated? Where your work is negated? Give examples. What do you do in these situations? Do others you know experience these challenges?

3. Across the nation there are many changes in expectations about the preparation and professional development of early educators. Have these changes impacted you? How have you responded to these changes? (Examples, earned a CDA or a college degree, took special courses, etc.).

4. Do you experience asymmetrical challenges as an early educator related to your language, ethnicity, race, or national origin? Do others you know experience these challenges? How have you or they handled them?

STEP 4: REASSESS YOUR WILLINGNESS TO FACE GOLIATH

What can **you** do now?

As you're reading Step 4, consider this question: Will you choose to bow out, hide out, or stake out?

You can out-distance that which is running after you, but not what is inside of you.

—Rwandan proverb

How do we face Goliath? As we approach Step 4, it is time to make a critical decision. If you decide to take on Goliath, you need to decide how to do it. Following our review of the realities (Step 1), the knowledge base (Step 2), and the impact of asymmetrical conflict (Step 3), will we, consciously or subconsciously, choose to end our journeys, to bow out? Will we choose to face Goliath as chameleons by hiding out, camouflaging ourselves when things get tough? Is it possible to simultaneously hide out while stealthily staking a claim to action? Or do we face Goliath head-on as a visible architect of change? Each individual makes this decision—and our collective behavior also reflects either de facto or intentional choices.

Bow Out

For many rational reasons, many of us choose to bow out. Face to face with the challenges, we spend most of our time complaining or feeling victimized by them. Many of us already work long hours—or second jobs—and have precious little time. Others of us believe that we lack the skill, knowledge, strength, or community to take action. And as we discussed in Step 3, still others are burdened by feelings of isolation, intimidation, or negation.

Facing Goliath as a Chameleon

Some of us choose to face Goliath as chameleons by camouflaging ourselves when things get tough. David, who initially put on a coat

47

of armor and a bronze helmet, eventually decided that such "camouflage" did not work for him.

What will we choose as early educators? Like David, we have put on the armor of our time: We have worked to increase communication, engagement, and collaboration with public education. We have focused understanding of children's transitions as babies and toddlers to preschool, then to elementary education. We are demonstrating our positions as "serious" educators who deserve a place at the table.

Is wearing this armor working for us? Without question, this approach has earned us some gains. We witness significant acceleration from a voting public that has made it clear that they support preschool.

How do we recognize when we or our colleagues are facing Goliath as chameleons? Being a chameleon often shows up when we reveal conflicting, or disingenuous, comments about current realities. In interviews, we hear statements that seem to be rooted in feelings of intimidation, negation, or isolation in the face of asymmetrical challenges, rather than in core knowledge or beliefs. We notice that the focus is on survival—repeating the words of "the other side" to appear to be a lesser target. This is how a chameleon responds, changing appearance as a type of social signaling, like the animal that uses camouflage in response to a predator.

How might wearing this full armor *not* be working well for many of us? Perhaps our definition of "education" is not fully aligned with public polls, and we have not well articulated what makes the early years distinctive. The evidence: more testing and less play for young children, more didactic and less constructivist pedagogical approaches, and an unbalanced emphasis on products rather than process.

Early educators are indeed creative! We have tried relentlessly to modify our pedagogy and wisdom to suit the educational trends of the day. We feel anxious as we try to be accommodating and adjust to rapid changes, even as we sometimes instinctively resist that change. At our core, some of us are not truly convinced that a sharp distinction between "education" and "child care" will serve children well. Yet as the funding environment changes, we adorn ourselves with chameleonlike colors in order to "Race to the Top" or to be sure that "No Child (is) Left Behind." In our hearts, though, many of us are not all in—many of us have not been convinced. And each day we come to work wearing the right colors but feeling anxious in them, while our inner voices scream out, "They just don't get it!"

But for now, we choose to hide out. Immobilizing fear can overwhelm, but it often goes unexpressed in honest terms, festering below the surface. As a result, others may interpret our behavior as complaining, or unreasonably resistant to change, without offering positive alternatives. Case in point: When reflecting with Valora Washington on her first year in office, a new state commissioner did not hold her tongue: "This field is full of whiners." Ouch!

Hiding Out in Plain Sight

We know our colleagues are wearing ill-fitting tunics when their comments are peppered with comments that illustrate these themes:

- A focus on compliance or completing checklists for survival;
- "Us" versus "them";
- Discomfort with what they are being asked to do, or ensure that others do; *and*
- A priority on raising funds from a certain initiative rather than excitement about the initiative itself.

But before we judge chameleon behavior too starkly, consider the story of Gwen (not her real name)—a seasoned educator and administrator. Gwen is a powerful, effective, and influential woman in her Latino community who has worked at high levels in many early childhood sectors. "Many people want to be loud and out front," she observes. "I keep a low profile." In response to the many early childhood initiatives that have come and gone over her decades of work, her team determines which initiatives are best for her community. "I pick my battles," she said. "I wait them out because I know they won't last. I adapt what they say to meet the needs of my community, but to the outsider it looks like I am complying."

Gwen operates from a strong core of knowledge about child development and developmentally appropriate practice. "We seek funding from every available initiative and then we do what has to be done" to sustain stability and continuity in her programs. A consummate networker, she maintains close ties with her grassroots community as well as with state and national policymakers.

Does she advocate for developmentally appropriate practice when she has concerns about various initiatives? "I just listen and let my work be the judge. Many times funders and policy folks are not truly open for dialogue. They are short-termers. We take the money and run. My commitment is to do what is best for my community."

Gwen's choices are intentional and exceptionally executed because of her very high level of skill and poise. Gwen's story indicates that, as a successful chameleon, she has analyzed her situation and has developed a strong understanding of the current realities facing her community. She advances through effective fundraising and intentional communication. She then decides to *act* as a chameleon. What would you do?

The chameleon amazes with its ability to change color—to appear invisible. But when we use the word chameleon to describe a person's actions, it's usually not in positive terms. We think, as Anne Morrow Lindbergh taught us: "The most exhausting thing in life, I have discovered, is being insincere."[24] Eventually David decided to remove the soldier's armor he was wearing, because it didn't suit him. He began his journey by being himself, by wearing his own colors. "I cannot go in these," he said. "I am not used to them."

Facing Goliath as Architects of Change

For us as early educators, the chameleon presents a conundrum: yes, of course, we must change. But we must do so with authenticity. Just as we cannot change because it suits others, we can't decide not to evolve. Unbending adherence to ages-old positions will be as unproductive as changing colors to look like a potential funder's dream recipient. Are we thoughtful and clear about what must be preserved and what losses we will endure? Our intent cannot be rigidity—it must be intentionality. After all, those who do not bend will break. So, we gradually realize: we might survive, but we certainly can't authentically thrive, as chameleons. What is the courageous and ethical choice for you individually—and for us, collectively?

Taking on Goliath as an architect of change requires planning and preparation, including:

- A willingness to engage in a process of deep and honest self-examination—an appraisal of beliefs, assumptions, and past actions;
- Honest evaluation of our work that enables us to distinguish those norms and values worth preserving from those that have become antiquated and dysfunctional;

- A collective intention to create a framework that defines early care and education and describes its programs and services; and
- Agreed-upon answers based on our own truth.

We must prepare to be uncomfortable through this. We will need to challenge our own cherished beliefs and acquire new knowledge and skills. We will need to rely on our character—our commitment, competence, courage, integrity, and wisdom. As architects of change, we cannot charge blindly into the fray. We must conduct ourselves with intelligence and creativity to outwit, outwork, and outlast Goliath. We will not help children without first being brave—equipping ourselves with intentional strategies—and being ready to act.

Are we bowing out, hiding out, or staking out our claim? The answer is important because, according to Will Durant, "We are what we repeatedly do."[25]

THEORIES ABOUT MOTIVATION

What makes someone willing to face Goliath—to step forward as an architect of change? Motivation theories help to explain what causes us to take action. Motivation is a force that initiates, guides, and maintains goal-oriented behaviors; the force could be biological, social, emotional, or cognitive in nature.

Evolutionary psychologists focus on the impact of genetics and heredity in motivating behavior. The incentive theory of motivation suggests that people are motivated to do things because of external rewards. According to the drive theory of motivation, people are motivated to take certain actions in order to reduce the internal tension that is caused by unmet needs, such as thirst.[26]

Humanistic theories of motivation, such as Abraham Maslow's hierarchy of needs, are based on the idea that people also have strong cognitive reasons to perform various actions. Maslow identified the basic needs that human beings have as, in order of their importance, physiological needs, safety needs, and the needs for belonging, self-esteem, and self-actualization.[27]

Later, David McClelland built on Maslow's work by identifying three learned motivators: a need for achievement, a need for affiliation, and a need for power.[28] Perhaps our dominant motivator influences whether we decide to hide out, bow out, or be an architect of change.

FIVE SMOOTH STONES

1. *Authenticity.* What is genuine for us? Being true to ourselves is fundamentally incompatible with hiding or seeming to go along, not make waves. David chose to be who he was, rather than dress in the ill-fitting clothes of the solider. We will look best and feel comfortable when we wear things that fit and flatter us!

2. *Beliefs.* What we believe matters. If we expect to fail, then we probably will. If we believe that we will overcome Goliath, we have already laid the blueprint for our success.

3. *Choices.* What do we do when faced with a tsunami of choices? Choosing to wear our "fake" colors might erode our effectiveness and accelerate the inevitability of decisions we do not want. Choosing to wear our "true colors" might make it more difficult for us to "get along." Take an honest reading of our true colors and remember to keep them at the forefront of your professional wardrobe.

4. *Names.* In the celebrated books by J. K. Rowling, Harry Potter and his friends refused to even say the name of their most dreaded enemy, Voldemort, for fear that he would hear and find them.[29] If we cannot say who or what our asymmetrical challenges are, we have no hope of prevailing over them. Is there a Goliath in our midst that is deemed so powerful that its name is rarely even spoken among us, and of even greater concern, no one dares to consider a challenge? Let's assemble and consider our own list of names.

5. *Erase.* From day to day and moment to moment, in the pressures of each interaction, we may make choices that we come to regret or realize were not the wisest. Erase them—and begin again. In some of our worst chameleon days, we might actually find ourselves saying things with conviction that directly contradict what we truly believe. (Did I say that?!) However, it's never too late to make amends, to change our practice, to learn more, to change.

REFLECT ON BECOMING AN ARCHITECT OF CHANGE
WHAT WOULD **You** DO?

ADVANCE! Plan and Prepare   Step 4: Reassess Your Willingness to Face Goliath

We all encounter times in our personal and professional lives when we make choices about how we will address our challenges.

1. At this moment in time, would you choose to bow out, hide out, or stake out your space to advocate for young children, their families, or our profession? Why?

2. Do you see examples of chameleon behavior within yourself or your colleagues? When does this occur and what are the consequences? What are the advantages and disadvantages of being a chameleon?

3. Do you see examples of architect-of-change behavior within yourself or your colleagues? When does this occur and what are the consequences? What are the advantages and disadvantages of being an architect of change?

ADVANCE!— Plan and Prepare

STEP 5: REVELATION—KNOW YOUR VISION AND IDENTITY

What can **you** do now?

As you read Step 5, think about how you would articulate a vision for your work and how you might contribute to creating a shared identity with your colleagues, both locally and nationally.

> All I'm saying is simply this: that all life is interrelated, that somehow we're caught in an inescapable network of mutuality tied in a single garment of destiny. Whatever affects one directly affects all indirectly. For some strange reason, I can never be what I ought to be until you are what you ought to be.
>
> —Martin Luther King[30]

Buoyed by a lifetime of clarity about his identity, David entered the stage with a vision of victory. He began with a vision, *even before any of the circumstances had changed.*

A vision declares and defines one's destiny, spoken bravely in the midst of unpleasant realities. (It's easy to espouse a vision when all is well and safe; it takes courageous commitment to speak of vision when you're standing toe-to-toe with a giant 10 times your size.)

Step 5 helps us Advance with insight and revelation about our core vision and identity as early educators. Opportunities begin to present themselves as we become clearer about who we are. In Step 5 we spend less time focusing on the problem and start spelling out the possibilities for consensus.

Recognizing that "We're caught in an inescapable network of mutuality tied in a single garment of destiny,"[31] our attention is drawn toward unity. Whatever affects one directly affects all indirectly. What do we want to create *together*? What results do we anticipate? With vision and shared identity, we believe we will find ways for our individual and sector intentions to cohere.

Reflecting on Your Intentions: Vision Starts Inside of You

As Bob Walls observed immediately upon accepting his new job, without a shared vision, Goliath seems insurmountable. As a new hire, Bob faced his realities:

> I watched a couple of school days and did a time study. I found out we were only spending maybe about an hour and 15 minutes on instruction and everything else was either recess or something else.

Bob knew that, in order to *Advance*, he had to change beliefs about what was possible, to build shared expectations for success despite circumstances of high community unemployment, poverty, and being designated as a failing school for a long time.

Having "no place to go but up," Bob Walls made his plan to advance with a very clear vision statement:

> At Campbell Elementary, we make no excuses for kids. No one here will be left behind. It makes no difference where our kids come from, they all deserve a chance. We have an obligation to have high expectations and to make sure children can reach those high expectations.

The implementation of this vision included a very strong commitment to add many preschool classrooms to the building. "We had no preschools here and I thought that had to change."

Walls fervently believes that "you aren't born a winner or a loser, you are born a chooser. We don't believe in 'bad kids.' . . . Our school has to be a beacon of hope . . . if a kid only gets one hug a day, it will be from us."

Reflection Is Required

Bob's efforts required every individual to reflect and decide for himself or herself if they could buy into this shared vision. "One of the first things that I did here was recognize that our teachers weren't talking to one another. So I gave them a common planning by grade levels and they visit other grade levels. My preschool people visit kindergarten.

My kindergarten teachers visit preschool. I had my 3rd- and 4th-grade classes adopt preschool classes. A big part of our success is that they talk to one another now." All of the work of the school program is interrelated.

Taking time to talk together—to reflect—can seem like a luxury, but we advance without it at our own peril. Leadership training and professional development—the contexts for reflection in most fields—can be hard to come by for early educators. We are so busy on the front lines that we rarely take the time to reflect. *This must change, starting now.*

Reflection can happen within groups or alone, formally (in professional development sessions) or informally (late at night, after dinner, with a notebook or journal), but the questions can be similar despite the context:

- What moved me to become an early educator?
- What still calls out to my heart and my mind?
- What brings me moments of joy in my daily work?
- What motivates me to stay in this work?
- What do I expect to happen?

Reflect on these questions thoroughly and specifically. Return to this "inner space" from time to time to confirm or adjust your professional development goals. When we feel comfortable opening ourselves up to personal exploration, we set the stage for honest exploration of our motives and goals. We identify areas for growth and learning (one of the hardest questions one can ask one's self is, "What *don't* I know?"). Self-reflection can fuel vitality, make room for renewal and intentionality, and eventually position us to be leaders with others. Reflection can confirm our future destiny and identity.

Choose to Buy-In: "We" and "They" Are All Early Educators

Cohering our personal selves into a shared professional identity has been a persistent challenge for early educators.[32] We work in many diverse settings—schools, child-care centers, Head Start programs, family child-care homes—with few opportunities to be physically together to even begin talking about our individual and collective identities. One would think that because we all focus on little children we would be prepared to play well in the sandbox together, but that simply isn't the case.

Early in her career, Valerie Gumes remembers belonging to a small, informal group of child-care providers, but "it was kept in a small circle . . . we had a better understanding of each other's struggles but the silos were the silos, and they were predicated by money."

One of the most daunting realities Marie Enochty faced was observing the unintended consequences of expanding public preschool on community-based programs. Sector relationships became tense. "The CAYL Institute helped me engage my early childhood program to understand the other side of the coin," she said: "Directors in private programs were laying blame on public schools for 'stealing' teachers with bachelor's degrees because they can make more money. Public school teachers retaliated by charging Head Start with not preparing their children for public schools. A blame game ensued, when the focus should have been on 'what the kids need next.'" Marie observed that the Head Start directors and school principals didn't even know one another, even though the programs were literally next door.

The truth is, among us, there is an "inescapable network of mutuality." In order to *Advance*, we must recognize our shared identity: we are all early educators.

Principal Jeff Wolff recalls his transition from an elementary school principal to a state director of the Head Start association:

> One of the first questions I asked was, "What relationship do you have with the public schools?" and the answer I was given was, "Not good." This is one reason I was hired. They felt that someone with a background in public schools might be able to make a better connection.

"We" and "they," or "us" and "them," emerged partly due to differences in history, funding, professional preparation, or our attitudes. These factors generate suspicion, create tension, and limit communication, creating the impression that we are more different than we are alike: hardly a "best practice" in the interest of children. We will be weaker than we need to be until we are bound by the fundamental, heartfelt conviction that we, together, can make young children's lives better.

As early educators, we have not yet created—for ourselves—that sense of shared professional identity. Yet, a shared professional identity could:

- Help us counter the feelings of isolation and low prestige,
- Allow us to lead together, not simply advocate for our own "branch of the tree," and
- Push us to define the attributes that make us who we are: our field's distinctive competencies, contributions, and capabilities that distinguish us from a good babysitter or loving grandmother.

In one model of building shared identity, the CAYL Institute organizes small groups of diverse leaders to work together on shared topical concerns (for example, dual language learners) to articulate both a challenge and a timely, relevant, and immediately actionable solution. Initially, leaders are excited about coming together with like-minded peers to prepare and plan . . . to do something. As the effort proceeds, however, the work of building consensus becomes more difficult than we might imagine. But we persevere, and eventually the effort invariably proves to be much more rewarding than imagined because the exercise gives participants a framework to address additional issues that they face.

Identity ABCs: Affiliate, Belong, Connect

Ultimately, the successful establishment of our identity depends on becoming part of the wider early care and education field—to connect to or belong to organizations and groups that support our collective work. Over the past decade, membership in nonprofit organizations, including many early childhood groups, has declined. Some, especially our younger colleagues, question the value of professional memberships. But at this critical juncture in the evolution of our field, we believe that membership in professional organizations is a responsibility, not a luxury.

Affiliation is essential for the sake of our mission, identity, and the families we serve. Connection with our fellow educators acknowledges the irrevocable tie between our self-interests and the interests of others.

- *The ABCs support our personal growth.* Early childhood professional organizations exist at every level of the profession, offering plenty from which to choose (see Figure 5.1). Employers don't usually require membership, but joining does send a signal that we regard our work as a profession. Volunteering in organizations provides the time and space to exercise our talents and develop new skills. Membership offers access to resources, job listings, and continuing education and credentialing, as well as introduction to new professional colleagues.
- *The ABCs keep us current with emerging knowledge.* Organizations often serve as conduits for new and best practices emerging from current research. They disseminate and publish new strategies and tools about supporting, instructing, engaging, and assessing the progress of young children in policy briefs and teaching tips. Organizations offer access to major journals, magazines, and newsletters and often hold regular conferences for discussing new knowledge and its application to practice. Industry news alerts us to new and upcoming legislative action that profoundly affects our work.
- *The ABCs build professional communities.* Early care and education organizations represent synergistic power—the potential of the *many* relative to the *one*. They generate mutual

Figure 5.1. Early Childhood Professional Organizations

- National Association for Family Child Care (NAFCC): www.nafcc.org
- National Association for the Education of Young Children (NAEYC): www.naeyc.org/membership
- Association for Childhood Education International (ACEI): acei.org/join-acei/join-acei.htm
- Child Care Aware of America: naccrra.org/membership-1
- Council for Exceptional Children: www.cec.sped.org/Membership
- Military Child Education Coalition (MCEC): www.militarychild.org
- National Black Child Development Institute (NBCDI): www.nbcdi.org/join
- National Head Start Association: www.nhsa.org/membership
- National Association of Early Childhood Educators: www.naecte.org
- Association for Early Learning Leaders: www.earlylearningleaders.org
- The World Forum: www.worldforumfoundation.org

support and sharing and forge avenues of communication. This power can be used to lobby for public policy that represents our view of the public good, for example.

Diane feels the power of the ABCs. "As a family child-care provider, I'm pretty much on my own. So I like to belong to groups and I try to network with other providers. If I didn't belong to those other groups or networks I might have missed the opportunity to learn about some of the things that are now big parts of my program."

Amy Mabbott also sees the value of bringing the various sectors together. "Last year we brainstormed a list of all the area preschools that feed into our district, and we formed this little consortium. We call it our book study group. We meet once a month and they have taught me so much about services in the area." By building new relationships, Amy plans and prepares to advance, personally and professionally.

Five Smooth Stones

1. *Identity.* I am an early educator. Yes, you are. Yes, we are.
2. *Vision.* We know what we want to create. We know what we are for—not just what we are against.
3. *Growth.* We need at least an annual jolt of professional development to stay plugged in: a course, conference, workshop, or seminar. What's on our calendar this year? Make time for growth. It might not be easy to schedule or to pay for, but it's worth it. Note to family child-care professionals: We deserve the same sense of healthy professional affiliation that comes from connecting with your peers. Our families will appreciate the fact that we are building our expertise, even if it is briefly inconvenient for them.
4. *Memberships.* Find a local, state, regional, or national organization that speaks to you—and join it. Better yet, don't just join—become actively involved.
5. *Unity.* Have we ever heard someone in our sector (such as family child care) criticize another sector of the field (such as Head Start)? With vision and unity in our cloth sack, we will want to examine those sentiments and explore the value of a mixed delivery system. Perhaps spend a day shadowing an early educator who works in a different setting—that is a strategy that is sure to raise our level of respect for it.

REFLECT ON BECOMING AN ARCHITECT OF CHANGE
WHAT WOULD You DO?

ADVANCE! Plan and Prepare   Step 5: Revelation—Know Your Vision and Identity

When we declare and define a vision, we have our "true north" and we map our destiny by it. When each individual knows in his or her heart, "This is my intention", it lights the path ahead.

1. Go back to the Step 1 reflection where you charted the realities that you face in your role as an early educator. In shaping your vision, how would you address your realities?

2. Articulate your vision.

3. What are your distinctive competencies as an early educator? What makes *you* a professional? What attributes distinguish you from a good babysitter or a loving grandmother?

4. How do you affiliate, belong, and connect to organizations and groups that share identity as early educators?

5. Refer to the "Where Early Educators Stand" figure in Step 2 and consider the ideas in Step 5. How do you see yourself relative to these ideas?

WHERE WE ARE SO FAR

In Chapter 2 we advanced our cause with planning and preparation. We took three more steps in our journey to become architects of change. We considered the notion of asymmetrical conflict and accepted that power is out of balance; paused to ask whether, considering the odds, we should enter the situation; and sought clarity about our vision and identity. Having prepared, it is now time to act, and Chapter 3 offers a path.

CHAPTER THREE

ACT!—Be Brave and Bold
What Would David Do?

David told King Saul that he would take action—that he would take on Goliath— but that he would do this in his own way, with his own skills, and using what he knew.

As early educators, what actions will we take? Chapter 3 brings us three steps closer to being the change agents we aspire to be. Action begins with Step 6: *we establish a Confidential Community and Share Leadership* in order to sustain ongoing support and coaching, and to engage our learning community in problem solving and reflection. Step 7 grounds us by centering our attention on everyday challenges— challenges that matter here and now. With Step 8, we act to align what we know with what we do.

Let's move ahead—and begin to act.

THEORY ABOUT CHANGE PROCESSES IN HUMAN SYSTEMS: TAKING ACTION

Kurt Lewin, often considered the father of social psychology, believed that to change our perspectives, we have to admit which of our old, useless, or counterproductive ideas are "frozen," work to "unfreeze" them so that we can accept new paradigms, then "freeze" these more enlightened beliefs so we can activate them in our work with young children.[1]

ACT!—Be Brave and Bold

STEP 6: JOIN A CONFIDENTIAL COMMUNITY AND SHARE LEADERSHIP

What can **you** do now?

As you read through Step 6, think about how you might create or expand your confidential community, determine your personal leadership traits, and build professional capital.

> It's the community in action that accomplishes more than any individual does, no matter how strong he may be.
>
> —Studs Terkel[2]

We might picture David as a heroic figure facing Goliath's challenge all alone, but we know that he felt—in an almost physical sense—the supportive arms of his community around his shoulders. He was not alone, and neither are we.

Perhaps the finest apparel we wear in stressful situations is the shawl of community, the warm embrace of shared vision and identity. We might find ourselves both surprised and gratified by the deep connections and common purposes we perceive as we develop our professional community. The CAYL Institute has frequently heard from early educators that the bonds and relationships that evolve in communities of practice are among their most valuable assets. These communities provide safety, support, and strength in numbers when facing asymmetrical challenges.

Examples of Growing in Community

Professional relationships help individuals and groups take important first steps to action, and they also help us persist in creating change and insisting on authentic, high-quality early care and education.

Amy Mabbott was the first principal in her district to incorporate a preschool program in her building, which left her feeling isolated. She "didn't have anybody to discuss" her challenges with, which prompted her to join a CAYL Institute network of local principals, educators, and administrators. She caught the community bug! Now, "We have a group that meets once a month" consisting of "preschool and kindergarten teachers in the area. We meet on our own after school."

Carrie Boyer understands the need of surrounding herself in a supportive community, but admits to a common challenge: It's difficult to commit the time it takes to build relationships. She also knows that such connections will offer her valuable leadership resources. "When we are at CAYL, it is wonderful to have discussions and to talk. Getting together with others in education does give me ideas to bring back to my school."

Bob Walls has learned to rely on, and lean on, a "community of learners and administrators who work together and talk together and share things. I know I can make a phone call to anyone . . . there's a network and there's trust behind that. Many of us are experiencing the same issues and someone else might have a creative solution that I could use or adapt. Some people say, well, you stole those ideas, but I say we share ideas . . . that's how you grow. The bottom line is what's best for kids. If it's a good idea, I'll take it."

Confidential community is also an antidote to the isolation that many early educators experience. "Sometimes you think you're an anomaly, you're in this boat by yourself and the things that don't come together the way they should are your fault. You think something only happens to you, but hearing others' experiences and how they solve problems keeps me learning," reflects Valerie Gumes. The CAYL Fellowship offered Valerie many opportunities to "Say what we truly thought openly . . . we were all somewhere on the learning curve," with different problems and insights. "We were able to share that knowledge and experience without having to put up shields," In the confidential community the educators could "go much deeper than the surface level, to hear other people's thinking . . . to affirm my decisions to believe what I believe."

Principal Chris Gibowicz adds:

What attracted me to the Fellowship was the collaboration and the camaraderie between principals. Because of the principal often being an isolated position, just being able to network with principals who are focused on early childhood was really beneficial for me. It has impacted my work. I have a network to call on if I have a question or people that are more like-minded.

Working in communities can reveal powers and abilities that we don't know we have. Space that is safe (physically, emotionally, and intellectually) can unleash creative thought, ideas, and concepts once considered unimaginable. We might find ourselves eager to lead in many ways, such as channeling the productive thinking of everyone in the group, offering strategies for tackling difficult tasks, facilitating the expression of everyone's ideas, or, at times, just being silent to let the creative impulses of others flow. Sometimes leading just means being still, appreciating the leadership qualities of others. In a more concrete sense, collaborative environments help us distribute the work that lies before us and balance the pressures across many shoulders in the strategic engagement process.

We might find ourselves belonging to a number of collaborative communities tucked within one another, like Ukrainian nesting dolls. We may have a small and immediate community consisting of the people with whom we work most closely and consistently. As we reach out and expand our network, we may find allies in the same or different sectors of the early care and education world. Ultimately, we may find ourselves feeling authentically connected to countless numbers of educators in the United States, which will lend power and urgency to the changes we are trying to enact. It is hard to exaggerate the power of community in finding voice, sharing ideas, gaining support, and building bridges.

Confidentiality Builds Trust

When beginning our work with groups, we establish principles of how we will work together so that everyone has clear expectations. Transparency facilitates the healthy dialogue we need to endure and move forward. We have found that groups, communities, or teams that do not invest up-front time to establish a framework for interaction often have to circle back when difficulties arise, and reset the group's working parameters.

Confidentiality is one example of a guiding principle for groups working together. It has certainly been heartily embraced in many professional learning communities we have encountered. CAYL Fellows frequently report that confidentiality is an expression of respect for people's courage in offering new ideas or critiquing the ideas of others. Consequently, confidentiality must exist for trust and respect to take root and thrive. A community that respects and offers confidentiality keeps our children and families, as well as our professional identity and core knowledge, at the center of our work. To value confidentiality is to practice humility, therefore lessening opportunities for the cult of personality or power dynamics to take root.

Building early educators' capacity to take risks is one of the benefits that Suzanne Federspiel observed in the culture of confidential community:

> Being in a Fellowship meant we were in a very safe community where we worked together and could try new ideas and see if they were good and defendable. It was safe to take risks. Having a trusting place to share experiences and innovative ideas is rare.

Principal Erin Pierce agrees:

> The ability to talk with colleagues and know that your conversation was not going to go anywhere is so important. Within my confidential community, we could be completely honest and bounce ideas off of one another and ask the hard questions that sometimes you feel uncomfortable asking within your district, because you don't want to admit, or aren't ready to let your district know, that something is a weakness for you and you need help.

When we engage in asymmetrical conflict, confidentiality is even more essential. Real dangers regarding job security and dissonance with people who have authority of position can create hesitancy and anxiety. At the CAYL Institute we respect the individual's right to privacy and honor the professional and personal relationships in which information is shared.

While CAYL's Fellowships honor confidentiality, CAYL Fellowships also work to increase members' skills and capacity for speaking up outside the safety of the group about the issues and needs of early care and education. To maintain confidence and the ability to share, participants agree to withhold identifying information about members when talking about the Fellowship with others.

Diversity: Look Beyond Your Comfort Zone

In addition to the focus on confidentiality, respect for diversity is one of the CAYL Institute's five key organizational principles.[3] The CAYL Institute exists for the purpose of bringing together sectors and populations to act with unity on behalf of our children and families, and for our profession. Therefore, The CAYL Institute acts affirmatively, mindfully, and with intention to invite varied voices to collaborate. Given the realities of race and class in our society, the CAYL Institute takes the time to develop relationships that make it comfortable and meaningful for others to join. The CAYL Institute recognizes that whether by sector, race, gender, or language, diversity still requires all of us to step outside of our comfort zone in order to disrupt silos and segregation (see Figure 6.1).

An intentional decision to embrace and heighten diversity has many benefits. It enables us to reach and better serve *all* children and families—and *all* early educators. It guarantees a multitude of voices and ideas and a wider representation of concepts and insights. It helps strengthen our knowledge base, filing the gaps. Amy Mabbott describes how confidential community strengthened her capacity to address diversity:

> I think the great thing about our confidential community is that, when I came from an inner-city district to a rural district, I really didn't think things would be that different, but the differences are huge. Just talking to other people about how they handle different situations is a huge benefit.

Diversity enriches the change agent who is willing to engage others with different perspectives than one's own, and to listen to every idea and viewpoint as a requirement for arriving at fair, equitable, and effective solutions. For early educators, an inclusive, curious mind is absolutely essential for being part of this increasingly complex, multilayered, global society and to earn the right to educate and nurture America's youngest citizens. (And let's face another reality: For the truly curious, working with and among people different from ourselves is a lot more interesting, stimulating, and eye- or mind-opening.)

Be Ready to Share Leadership

Confidential communities and diversity must precede truly shared leadership, and people must be open to giving, receiving, accepting, and valuing critical feedback about their ideas and concerns. Trust leads to openness, openness invites authentic shared leadership, and from that leadership comes solutions and sustained social change. Knowing this, every CAYL cohort is designed to include people from different sectors—and different racial, ethnic, gender, and language

Figure 6.1. Promoting Leadership Diversity—How Do We Begin to S.H.A.R.E.?

1. SEE. Are people who reflect the diversity of our community actually present and represented in meetings on important program, policy, or professional issues? What critical disparate outcomes exist for young children and families in my community? Are certain ethnic groups excluded from leadership or relegated to certain roles? When my group wants to hear the viewpoint of (fill in the group), do we always call on (fill in the individual's name)? Are there any patterns we haven't noticed before?

2. HEAR. Are there any important stakeholders who we do not hear from routinely? Would I be surprised to hear what some of my colleagues really think and experience? How might cross-cultural dialogues or communication training be useful in my professional community? How can individuals and organizations learn to listen to different voices with respect?

3. ASK before you act. How can I—and my organization—be a catalyst for change? Are there others interested in questions of diversity? What might we do with—not for—others? Are we willing to bridge boundaries of race, class, and gender? How do the values of social justice, equity, and inclusion intersect with my beliefs about our profession? What is my theory of change? What actual policy, program, or personal development goals do I have?

4. REFLECT. Am I aware of the cultural contexts in which I, my colleagues, families served, and others in my environment exist? How can attention to diversity help to achieve my organizational, professional, and personal goals? How do I plan to address any discomfort or unease that I may experience in this learning process? To what extent has my organization engaged in cultural self-assessment of its policies, structures, and staff attitudes or practices?

5. ENGAGE. Are there colleagues with whom I might engage in a discussion? Does my program meaningfully involve consumers, stakeholders, and key constituency groups? Has our organization or group created alliances and partnerships with leaders from community-based organizations or cultural institutions who have complementary goals or who serve the families we serve? How are these allies involved in designing, as well as in implementing, initiatives together with us? Do I have a long-term commitment to realize the desired outcomes?

Source: Washington, 2007.

communities are placed in situations where they get to know one another and share leadership on a common cause. Although intergroup acquaintance is very common today (who doesn't have a Black, Irish, Latino friend?), even today, too many of us remain isolated by racial communities. We are struck by how much work still needs to be done to encourage, model, and realize authentic diverse relationships.

In shared leadership there is no one hierarchical leader. Over the life of a project, there may be serial, distributed, or multiple points of leadership in which people broadly share power and influence. It is unlikely that one person could provide the necessary leadership, expertise, passion, or experience to handle every issue or requirement.

In our CAYL circles, there are two levels of responsibility: We all must complete the specific tasks and roles assigned to us, or for which we volunteered, and we all own a measure of responsibility for our initiatives' overall outcomes and success, or failure. The pleasant irony here is that each person in the group has equal power over the others *and* equal need for support from the others.

Shared leadership also gives each of us some "elbow room" for risk-taking, innovation, and commitment. Alone, many of us hesitate or fail to contradict the ideas or beliefs of a powerful internal or external Goliath, or to offer an idea that, on the immediate surface, might look or sound "crazy."

This hesitancy can paralyze the individual, but it can also stop the progress of the group in its tracks. In the vacuum of silence, new ideas never get the chance to breathe and grow. Shared leadership requires a freely flowing environment of critical collegiality (where people feel free to espouse their ideas and their colleagues feel free to critique them honestly, with respect and appreciation).

When discussing leadership in focus groups and informal discussions, people often ask us if Valora Washington is the leader of the CAYL subject matter, policy, or issue groups. The answer is a resounding "no." Leadership is a community attribute, and the community is a source of strength and insight. Participants work in subject-matter or issue-focused teams to analyze, advance, and act on a program or policy issue that matters to them. Valora and other CAYL leaders facilitate and serve as coaches for the work of the teams. They ask questions and reinforce shared purpose, recognizing shared leadership, keeping the team focused on creating "timely, relevant, and immediately actionable" policies or interventions, building networks for social support, and encouraging members who may have difficulty articulating their views to exercise their voices.

This approach fosters democratic leadership, promotes egalitarian principles, and strengthens a group's self-determination and participation. Such leadership requires ownership, learning, and sharing from many directions.

We understand that this focus on shared leadership can sound idealistic, even naïve. The truth is that shared leadership can be complex and quite difficult, but when done effectively, it can propel impact and results. We have participated in groups that worked through mountains of occupational rhetoric and academic jargon to uncover the core issues. Every group has to fill its knowledge gap in different ways. Both the naturally talkative or energetic and the reticent and cautious must examine their collaboration skills. Agreement on the analysis and approach to action is often hard-won. This work is intense, sophisticated—and absolutely doable.

Guiding principles such as confidentiality, diversity, and shared leadership cannot be simply accepted as "givens"—they must be articulated, preferably in writing, and encoded into a professional learning community's charter, mission statement, or principles of interaction.

Here are a few examples of impact by Fellows, using the tenets of confidential community, diversity, and shared leadership: One group of Fellows convinced their state to begin counting early educators by gender as a step toward promoting more men in the workforce; another group ultimately convinced the state to include a module on cultural diversity in state trainings; and many others collaborated to encourage the early childhood community to explore, and the state to eventually develop, a Quality Rating and Improvement System. Many of these beginning policy and program efforts are rooted in larger visions (surely one module on cultural competence does not make one competent), but the learning process and new networks continue to evolve into broader, sustained spheres of influence.

Another example of collaborative work impacted 52,000 children in Massachusetts who received child-care vouchers. The Bessie Tartt Wilson Initiative for Children (BTWIC) took on the everyday challenge of discontinuous child care for families who, typically in most states, received a 6-month certification period. If a parent's income status changes by any amount, no matter how small (as it frequently does for mobile families), a child's voucher is discontinued.[4] This troubles early educators, who know that continuity of care is critical for vulnerable children. The BTWIC led the charge in collaboration with many others, successfully convincing the state to make a change. Massachusetts now has a policy of providing a 1-year voucher that allows for continuity of care, better funding stability for providers, higher-quality programs, and greater access and affordability for families.

THEORY ABOUT CHILD DEVELOPMENT: CONTINUITY OF CARE

This chapter describes early educators advocating for changes in the child-care subsidy system based on the principle of *continuity of care*. Continuity of care refers to ways of organizing child life, or children's transitions, to maximize "secure" attachments and minimize disruptions, or anxious, avoidant, or ambivalent attachments. A strong theoretical framework for this concept of continuity of care is attachment theory, from the work of John Bowlby[5] and Mary Ainsworth and colleagues.[6]

In sum, this research finds that secure attachment relationships offer protection and security for children, and that extended time is needed to develop these relationships. One way for early care and education programs to promote continuity of care is to allow the children to stay with a primary caregiver for an extended period of time – a rare practice nowadays even though we know that children may experience a sense of loss and depression when their bonds with significant adults are continually broken (as often happens with high staff turnover). As early educators we respect our knowledge base, and align what we know with what we do when we remove policy or administrative barriers to attachment, including staff turnover.

Build Professional Capital

As we accelerate our efforts through confidential communities, we build what Michael Fullan and Andy Hargreaves call the "professional capital" needed for teacher fulfillment and effectiveness. Observing the decline of the teaching profession in the United States, Fullan and Hargreaves found in international studies that successful countries develop the *whole* profession. This means requiring teachers to be:

> Highly committed, thoroughly prepared, continuously developed, properly paid, well-networked, and capable of making effective judgments together using all their capabilities and experience . . . you can't accumulate much human capital by focusing only on the capital of individuals. Human capital must be complemented by social capital . . . a good team, school, or system lifts everyone. As we often see in sports, higher individual human capital, a few brilliant stars, does not necessarily improve the overall team. When the vast majority of teachers possess the power

of professional capital, they become smart and talented, committed and collegial, thoughtful and wise. Those few colleagues who persistently fall short of the mark eventually will not be tolerated by peers who see them as letting down their profession and students.[7]

In contrast, the system in the United States uses:

Strategies of rewarding or punishing individual teachers with measures like test-driven, performance-based pay or concentrate their energies on the extremes of competence with gushing teacher-of-the-year ceremonies or gung-ho proposals to remove the bottom 5% of educators from classrooms.[8]

Be Inspired!

Can you help build our professional capital? Join a confidential community and share leadership? *We believe you can!* We are also convinced that everyone has the capacity to be a change-maker, to accelerate change. Our field now requires us to democratize social change by building open and inclusive spaces to share, learn, and collaborate on new approaches to creating impact. Start by thinking about others with whom you might develop these relationships. Reflect on examples of shared leadership that you have already witnessed. Be inspired by the leadership you see in others.

Prepare to accelerate change!

FIVE SMOOTH STONES

1. *Respect.* Respect is at the heart of our effectiveness as architects of change. In everything we do, we treat people with courtesy, politeness, and kindness. We practice the Golden Rule.
2. *Trust.* We earn trust by being trustworthy, reliable, and consistent. We give trust when we are willing to abide by group decisions, even when we are not present. Trust is the foundation of shared leadership.
3. *Confidentiality.* We keep our mouths shut. We can be trusted with the intimate expressions shared by others. We encourage others to express opinions and ideas, and we hold their expressions in confidence. A confidential atmosphere is one of great freedom and safety. We can learn more in this space.
4. *Collaboration.* We work well with others. We care about their interests and treat their passions with respect. We know that big

results are possible when we combine forces with others. We listen to and incorporate the suggestions of others.

5. *Diversity.* We recognize and honor differences. We are inclusive. We pay attention to who is missing at the table and extend invitations to others.

REFLECT ON BECOMING AN ARCHITECT OF CHANGE
WHAT WOULD **You** DO?

ACT! Be Brave and Bold   Step 6: Join a Confidential Community and Share Leadership

Many early educators report deep satisfaction growing out of the relationships and sense of common purpose they have developed in their professional communities. Strength in numbers is significant. Never walk alone!

1. Do you have a confidential community?

    a. Make a list of your trusted colleagues.

    b. How does your confidential community support your practice and ongoing development as an early educator?

2. If you don't have a confidential community, brainstorm actions you can do right away that will help you to build one with other early educators. Be sure to consider how you might make it diverse and inclusive.

3. Cite examples of how you interact with or share leadership with others. Who or what inspires you?

4. Describe a situation where shared leadership—in the classroom, with families, or with other early educators—has led to a successful outcome. What lessons did you learn?

ACT!—Be Brave and Bold

STEP 7: BEGIN WITH YOUR EVERYDAY CHALLENGES

What can **you** do now?

As you read through Step 7, consider the kinds of everyday challenges you encounter in your work and think about the suggested "four agreements" as a way of overcoming those challenges.

Learn the rules like a pro, so you can break them like an artist.

—Pablo Picasso

Can you feel it? We're picking up speed and moving ahead.

So, where do we begin? What issues should we tackle first? One answer comes from the advice of Booker T. Washington: "Cast down your bucket where you are."[9] Begin with your everyday challenges—our current, existing realities, the issues and situations we see every day. Starting with our everyday challenges—the pragmatic, hands-on applications of real-time problems—gives us the rough terrain we need to get our footing and gather speed.

Reflecting on our everyday challenges can be a formidable yet deeply satisfying task. Why do everyday challenges seem so hugely challenging? Perhaps it's their very immediacy that requires us to breathe deeply: There is nowhere to run! We know the challenge, we've decided to engage with it, and we have strengthened our core knowledge about how to deal with it. But the familiarity of the challenges we know makes it possible for us to take some level of action—even if it is to crawl, or take baby steps, before walking and running. Zig Ziglar says: "You don't have to be great to start, but you have to start to be great."[10]

We at CAYL have had conversations with hundreds of early educators about their dreams for young children and the role of early educators. The harsh realities of inequities for children, and for the staff, come bursting forth along with expressions of deep passion and commitment to this work. "Somebody should do something about it!" is a common refrain. But when the question gets turned around—"Why don't you do something?"—there is silence or mumbling or questions. "How could we get started?"

In almost every story, we recognize that the speaker could have done something to make a difference—it's getting started that seems to be the challenge, a seemingly insurmountable barrier.

Getting started takes more energy than you might imagine. A 10-day space shuttle mission uses 83% of its fuel in the first 2 minutes. Nearly 96% of the weight of a space shuttle is equipment built just to get it off the ground.[11] We are not unlike that space shuttle!

The irony of getting started is that it takes as much power to not act—to worry, overthink, dream up excuses—as it does to take the first steps toward action. Asymmetrical power can be used to constrain human action (Goliath used quite a lot of it to make David's community cower, doubt, delay), and, quite often, we are the ones exerting power to keep ourselves from acting. We must call upon our courage and stop overestimating Goliath's power while underestimating our own power. Anything we do to get started in taking action is a stepping-stone toward progress. After all, what you don't start today can never be finished tomorrow.

Identifying Your Everyday Challenges

Finding opportunities to be architects of change is not difficult if we pay attention to what we see in our everyday environments and make a decision to ACT! You might recognize an everyday challenge because it recurs consistently and chronically; it is something that presents itself on a regular basis or over an extended period of time. (This is different from a crisis—a problem that can erupt suddenly and on a large scale). Some suggest that chronic problems cause us far more stress than the occasional crisis because we live with our chronic problems in a cumulative way.

Choose a problem that is close to you, one that you see constantly. Keep it simple. Don't try to accomplish too much too soon. Cut out everything that is unnecessary. Start small and build over time. This makes your goal specific and manageable. A goal you think is achievable also strengthens your motivation to accomplish it. You will genuinely want to succeed because it matters in your daily life.

Carrie Boyer and her staff faced a critical everyday challenge: the variety of literacy levels in their classrooms, which, she says, makes them feel like their jobs are "10 times harder." Having enacted a policy of no kindergarten retention, Carrie worked to assign assistants in each kindergarten class, and to hire an intervention specialist.

Like Carrie, something is bothering you and the issue just isn't going to go away. Instead of denying the reality of the issue, let that concern mature in your thinking. Articulate an idea about something in which you have some expertise and passion, and start creating change strategies around that idea. Find others who share your passion and exchange potential strategies with them.

Realize that after you set your goal, events may happen that you cannot predict, so plan to be flexible and make adjustments. The more you make *starting* a habit, the easier it will be for you next time. Remind yourself that your efforts matter, regardless of the outcome. The experience of trying can even be an opportunity to learn. You have a voice, an idea, and some level of ability—that's really all you need to begin to face Goliath. Goliath is not all-powerful and you are not powerless.

How Do We Get Started?

First, we start by recognizing that Goliath is not all-powerful, and that we are not powerless. Then, we look around us and ask questions about our Goliath. Next, we are inspired by the courageous actions of others. Finally, we follow the four agreements as a way to establish guidelines for any action we may take.

First: Recognize That Goliath Is Not All-Powerful: We Have Power, Too! We must call upon our courage and accept that Goliathan challenges can be overcome. Fear of stepping outside of our comfort zone entraps us with fear of failure. But almost always, failure isn't fatal; a "failure" could be the fastest way to accelerate your success. The inventor Thomas Edison said it best: "I have not failed. I've just found 10,000 ways that didn't work."[12]

Many times early educators believe that someone else—someone better known, more qualified, or in a more authoritative position—can or will make the change. This belief is simply a form of intimidation (self-inflicted, but intimidation nevertheless). If we've had that thought, we advise ourselves: get over it. Step outside of any self-imposed boundaries and take the first steps toward change—preferably with a confidential community of your own. Remember, the change we seek will require distributive, adaptive leadership—leadership by everyone.

Principal Carrie Boyer also faced the "all-powerful" everyday challenge of staff blaming the children's socioeconomic status, national origin, or lack of language proficiency for their poor educational outcomes. Carrie asked teacher peer groups to sit down and formulate a plan, child by child: "What interventions can we provide? Do we need a speech pathologist? An intervention specialist? Does an instructional assistant need to work with this child more often?" Carrie said the staff members have finally stopped saying, "We can't." "We're learning how to connect well with all students and how to adapt teaching methods to each student when possible."

Second: Look Around You and Ask Questions. Sometimes the first step is not the most obvious step. Putting a bucket under the leak in the roof will keep the floor dry, but it won't fix the leak. The first step might be to ask a question: Where *is* that hole in the roof? Information is important. So let's look around and ask ourselves, and others, many questions:

- What exactly is the problem?
- Can I state it as a question?
- What do I already know about this problem?
- What would I like to find out about this problem?
- What solution do I want to create?
- What are options for action?
- Who can I engage to help me?
- What are the next three things I could do to get started?

We use these questions to closely examine our everyday challenges and to face Goliath at its root.

Third: Be Inspired by the Courageous Actions of Others. Let's give ourselves time to determine the action steps we should take to address our everyday challenge. Be specific about each new step we will take, the obstacles we're likely to encounter, and how we will face the Goliath in front of us. Be inspired by the courageous acts that we see in the work of others. And remember that seemingly small efforts can make a big difference, as Kitt Cox found out when he faced one of his everyday challenges.

Kitt, an administrator with the Massachusetts Family Networks, noticed a big problem in his town:

People don't generally know this, but the incidence of diaper rash went way up when the Great Recession first hit in 2008.

Poor families were trying to save money. So we had a diaper drive and the family networks were giving diapers away. We did this with a grassroots-style public relations campaign. Because we are so tied to families, and to the people and groups that support them, we were naturals for getting the word out. And word of mouth is a powerful way to convince people and create a culture of caring— doing something. The tag line for the diaper drive was "When something stinks, it's time for a change." You have to keep your sense of humor.

Indeed!

Within early care and education communities, we see endless examples of fresh leadership solving everyday challenges by courageous action and commitment carried forward in unexpected and wonderful ways. Three examples:

1. *Every day we see poor transition between settings such as child care and public schools.* The Boston, Massachusetts Countdown to Kindergarten initiative started as a concern among Boston Children's Museum staff who were listening to the worries of Head Start families. Countdown is now a major, multifaceted, citywide effort that reaches out to families to make registering children for kindergarten:

> Clear and simple! The easy to follow Countdown 5-4-3-2-1 Steps will guide you through the year-long process of visiting and selecting schools, registering for school, meeting your assigned school, getting ready for school over the summer, and starting school in the fall. We also connect you to many fun social and learning activities and resources that you can share with your child to help him or her get ready to thrive in school. Remember, you are your child's first teacher![13]

2. *Every day we see families of infants and toddlers who worry about what to expect in schools.* Growing out of Countdown to Kindergarten, Play to Learn Playgroups[14] bring together parents, children under 3 years old, and an early childhood professional to build a community of peers that fosters nurturing behaviors, helps families access needed services, and models developmentally appropriate practice. Playgroups help schools become community resources where parents are welcome and to which they can turn for needed support. Introducing babies and toddlers and their families to the school through weekly playgroups makes families feel comfortable and part of the school community, and helps a school's staff strengthen their connections to families.

3. Every day we see practice that is not consistent with our knowledge base. Courageous school leaders in the Mahoning Valley of Ohio decided to get serious about using the research evidence as it applies to two policies: kindergarten retention and screening children out of kindergarten on the basis that they were "not ready." Although the state of Ohio spent $43 million in 2006 on grade retention for nearly 8,000 children in kindergarten through 3rd grade,[15] early educators recognized that keeping children home for another year was not going to help them. Here, early educators assigned themselves to this challenge and cast down their buckets where they were in order to tackle this everyday challenge. They watched, listened, and figured it out—and demonstrated their ability to align knowing with doing to effect change.

When he agreed to lead one of the poorest schools in Ohio with very low achievement levels, Bob Walls knew that family and community engagement were essential to a turnaround.

> I'm constantly in contact with parents. We overwhelm our families with welcome . . . please come, please come! We can't do this without you.

Every week Bob sends an e-newsletter to families with stories about the good things that have happened at school. He began family fun nights and offered incentives for parents coming to important meetings. He admits that some of the new initiatives for increasing parent involvement were not particularly popular with his staff, but he knew they must be done to better the lives of his students.

A second everyday challenge Bob tackled was the low level of student achievement, especially in literacy. "We decided to spend at least 85% of our time on reading and literacy strategies because there's only so much anyone can achieve academically and in life without being able to read." Children may now come in before school hours and after school for extra study or reading with a staff member. Bob began to see results and started using the improved achievement data to build teacher morale. "You have to show teachers that they are an important part of the process; once you show them the small victories, that they have an impact, they start believing in themselves."

The school has adopted the slogan "One more minute on task, one more day, one more hour, or one more student," because 2 years in a row, the school missed their math achievement goal by one student. Bob told his staff, "If we had worked one more minute with that student or one more hour, maybe we could have made it." We, too, can "cast down your bucket" and get started on everyday challenges.

In their book *Critical Thinking: Learn the Tools the Best Thinkers Use*, Richard Paul and Linda Elder remind us that most of us have great capacity to see and develop solutions to the challenges we experience in everyday life. But most of the time, our capacity lies dormant, undeveloped, and inactive.[16] Improving life for young learners and advancing early learning is like improving our ability to play piano or soccer: It takes practice. Building our strength and acuity, as architects of change, will require focused attention and conscious commitment to learn about the tasks at hand, and most importantly, to take the steps necessary to act upon it constructively. Wishing to play the piano is ineffective. One plays piano well as a result of creating the habit of practice over days, weeks, months, and years.

Follow the Four Agreements

To begin with your everyday challenges, take the action necessary to get started—and practice, practice, practice! Here, we borrow gratefully from Don Miguel Ruiz's 1997 book *The Four Agreements*, a meditation based on the ancient Toltec wisdom of the native people of southern Mexico. The Four Agreements suggests a conceptual framework to ground your approach to action as you face your everyday challenges:

Agreement 1. Be impeccable with your word—Speak with integrity. Say only what you mean. Avoid using the word to either gossip or to speak against yourself.

Agreement 2. Don't take anything personally—What other people say or do has nothing to do with you. When you are immune to the opinions and actions of others, you won't be the victim of needless intimidation, negation, or isolation.

Agreement 3. Don't make assumptions—It takes courage and integrity to ask questions and to express what you really want. Strive to avoid misunderstandings.

Agreement 4. Always do your best!—Our children and families—and our colleagues—want and deserve your very best.[17]

FIVE SMOOTH STONES

1. *Priorities.* With so many Goliaths—and so many stones—how do we get started? Being able to set priorities is the key to getting organized and making the most of our time. We know that setting priorities leverages our ability to be successful.

2. *Consultations.* We are open to consultation because we value the exchange of opinions, the wisdom of experts, and new sources of information. Using the wisdom of others expands our reach.

3. *Awareness.* Early educators: it's time to wake up! We are not sleep-walking through our careers, nor are we simply holding jobs. Goliath is not all-powerful. We have power as long as we are alive to the needs and potential of our children, our families, and ourselves!

4. *Actions.* We analyze our current realities, but they do not paralyze us. We are not waiting for perfect conditions before we can get started on our vision. Nor are we seeking an immediately big result, viewing anything less with skepticism. We face our everyday challenges with everyday actions. As Dr. Martin Luther King Jr. said, "Take the first step in faith. You don't have to see the whole staircase, just take the first step."[18]

5. *Questions.* To ask the right questions, we first need to know what we really need to know. Asking the right questions is key to problem solving—and we often do not ask the right questions. Our questions are not: Who should be blamed? Who did what wrong? Why is this happening? Ursula K. Le Guin says, "There are no right answers to wrong questions."[19] However, questions should frame our initial approach: How can we clearly define the problem? What do we know about it? Are there solutions that others have used successfully? What seems feasible in this situation? Questions matter.

REFLECT ON BECOMING AN ARCHITECT OF CHANGE
WHAT WOULD **You** DO?

ACT! Be Brave and Bold   Step 7: Begin with Your Everyday Challenges

Select an everyday challenge you want to work on and think about it systematically. Ask yourself:

1. ANALYZE! What exactly is the problem? Can I state it as a question?

2. ADVANCE! What do I already know about this problem? What would I like to find out about this problem? What can I learn about this problem? What information is needed to interpret and analyze the problem?

3. ACT! What is the most obvious response? What solution do I want to create? What are options for action? What are strategies to change the situation?

4. COMMUNITY and SHARED LEADERSHIP: Who can I engage to help me?

5. What are the next three things I could do, alone or working with others, to get started to change this problem?

STEP 8: ALIGN WHAT WE KNOW WITH WHAT WE DO

What can **you** do now?

As you read Step 8, think about how you will learn from criticism; assess your commitment, competence, and courage; and examine patterns of action that you can use to align what you know with what you do.

You are what you do, not what you say you'll do.

—C. G. Jung[20]

David knew he could conquer Goliath because, as a shepherd, he had faced other kinds of Goliaths. But he did so without wearing "ill-fitted clothes"—traditions and practices that others would impose upon him. He was comfortable with the slingshot, a tool he had built himself. Wisely, he chose to align what he already knew with what he had to do next.

Neither can we, as early educators, walk in ill-fitting clothes. Step 8—our decision to act in alignment with what we know—is a decision to focus on our collective integrity. Defined by Scott L. Carter, integrity is "the courage of our convictions [and] the willingness to speak and act on behalf of what we know is right."[21] Step 8—our quest for alignment—has two tasks: Embrace qualities of character that support us in the work of alignment; *and* take actions that help us achieve alignment. Step 8 requires integrity—and character.

Building Character from Aha! Moments

A willingness to speak and act—to build our character—is often an outcome of the steps we take as we face Goliath. Facing our realities, and reflecting on our vision and identity, we often have a sudden insight, realization, awareness, or comprehension about our work that we did not have before. Who hasn't had an aha! moment of alignment—a time when the strength of our convictions is tested in the face of asymmetrical conflict? Valerie Gumes describes her aha! moment:

I wasn't interested in becoming a really strong advocate until circumstances started to challenge my knowledge of what a leader is. It turns out I do have to be a strong advocate so I can talk about my kids' needs. This is my community. I grew up here. We've invested a lot in knitting together a community that cares for its children. I didn't become an education leader to let all this data collection and testing take over our early childhood programs. I'm using my seniority and position to take more risks and push harder against any practices that are just the wrong thing for our children and communities.

While external forces can be responsible for misalignments and aha! moments, sometimes aha! moments stem from the reality that the misalignment can come from within, as Mary Fran Jones illustrates:

I was starting my 39th year and becoming quite settled. I say this apologetically: You start to think that the kids are coming to you "not ready." It was an absolute and complete paradigm shift on my part to become aware that it's not the children who needed to be ready for our school, but we needed to be ready to meet the children where they were in their academics and socialization. I was looking for that magic answer—how to fix kids. A willingness to change your mindset is absolutely huge.

The Brave and the Bold: Ready for Rebuke?

Whether the quest for alignment originates from internal or external forces, it usually reveals tension. Our colleagues, supervisors, or funders may not embrace the change. Staff and families in our program might resist alternative or unfamiliar approaches. Even David's brother questioned and accused David: "Why have you come down here? And with whom did you leave those few sheep in the desert? I know how conceited you are and how wicked your heart is; you came down only to watch the battle." A tongue-lashing like that could discourage any of us!

Criticism should be considered honestly and fearlessly. We must face rebuke because when fair and true, it helps us grow. With unfair criticism, we can see the facts for what they are and move forward without the burden of guilt or doubt. Ignoring criticism is as counterproductive as accepting undeserved censure.

Where did David get the brave, bold spirit to face criticism square on, assess it honestly, and move forward unburdened by unfair attacks? How did he persevere through seemingly insurmountable obstacles?

In Step 8 we embrace three personal qualities of character—commitment, competence, and courage—as factors that enable change agents to begin their work, to be brave and bold. Character combines knowing and practicing what is right to engender trust. We exhibit character through behaviors—we follow through on commitments, lead by example, and do the little things well. Self-discipline, determination, moral strength, and ethical conduct express our character to others and ourselves. These behaviors and habits reflect the inner strength of character that allows us to pursue the change we seek, to be standard-bearers for our profession.

Courage: What's Love Got to Do with It? Maya Angelou tells us: "Courage is the most important of all the virtues because without courage, you can't practice any other virtue consistently."[22] It takes a lot of courage to let go of the old and embrace something new and not yet secure. *Cour* means heart; the original definition of the word was to tell your story with your whole heart. Clearly naming and facing our performance and credibility gaps can be a profound act of love that gives us the power to act. "Love is an expression of power," says Ericka Huggins. "We can use it to transform the world."[23] Indeed! "Power without love is reckless and abusive," adds Martin Luther King Jr., "and love without power is sentimental and anemic."[24] How could we dare express passion for children and families without courage to act?

As individuals and as professionals, we can begin to call forth our inner courage by consciously nurturing an awareness that courage exists within us, tackling small challenges, risking change. When we come to work with courage as a tool, we can lead and not be led.

Commitment. David McNally teaches that "Commitment is the enemy of resistance, for it is the serious promise to press on, to get up, no matter how many times you are knocked down."[25] When we commit to act on behalf of children, families, and ourselves, we pledge to engage ourselves in the challenge, even though it is asymmetrical. Commitment is a sign that we have our words, our hearts, and our intentions in our hands, and that we are ready for the responsibilities that this requires. Goals, no matter how lofty, cannot be achieved without the commitment to achieve them. And commitment comes from within you.

Knowledge and practice cannot align without personal commitment. Our passion and commitment motivate discovery and validation. They lie at the heart of why we became early educators, and because our commitments involve children, the public expects them to be exercised with integrity. Wavering commitment appears as no commitment at all, a challenge quickly discovered by the chameleon. As William Shedd points out, "A ship is safe in harbor, but that's not what ships are for."[26]

Competence. A courageous and committed person without competence will find it difficult to be a standard-bearer. "Competence without virtue is poisonous," state Daniel Taylor and Mark McCloskey. "It simply makes one more effective at doing wrong."[27] "If you want to be successful," Will Rogers advises, "It's just this simple: Know what you're doing. Love what you are doing. And believe in what you are doing."[28]

What is competence in our field of work? Education and employment requirements for early educators vary state by state and depend on the program setting or employer.[29] Based on the research on the realities young children face, we must face our own sobering reality: Some of us are doing the wrong things with children. A major challenge for many of us is to define the skills and abilities that early educators should minimally demonstrate.

Building collective competence takes time and is rarely easy. Identifying developmentally inappropriate teaching at her school, Principal Carrie Boyer noticed, "The children do a lot of sitting, paper/pencil activities. I see a lot of 'I do, you do' type of teaching. The teachers think the kids need to adjust." Carrie said part of the problem is that some teachers have done things this way for a long time and it's hard for them to change. Sometimes, Carrie believes, the teachers listen to what she recommends and start "yes ma'aming," her, or saying they've changed their approach, but haven't really done so. "The attitude is 'I go in my room, close my door, and do what I want.'"

Sometimes the staff are more ready for change than the administrator. When Principal Jeff Wolff joined the CAYL Fellowship, he was a bit stunned by the initial reaction of his kindergarten teacher. "I didn't know you were interested in that," she said. Recognizing that he needed to learn more, Jeff connected with community-based programs, brought experts to his school for professional development, and participated in the Tools of the Mind[30] pilot project.

Increasing collective competence was a major factor in change at Campbell Elementary for Bob Walls:

> We started by making sure that teachers got professional development. We put them through all kinds of trainings. We wanted to get out of academic watch. At the end of the 1st year we met AYP. The 3rd year we were rated excellent.[31] And the morale skyrocketed because then they had a direction. They knew where to go, they knew what to do.

We agree with Robert Kennedy's belief in ripples of hope! Hope springs from numerous diverse demonstrations of character—acts of courage, commitment, and competence that shape our destiny. Each time someone "stands up for an ideal or acts to improve the lot of others, or strikes out against injustice, he sends forth a tiny ripple of hope, and crossing one another from a million different centers of energy and daring those ripples build a current that can sweep down the mightiest walls of oppression and resistance."[32]

Brave and Bold: Patterns of Action for Goliathan Challenges

Tiny ripples of hope spur us to action. Our second task in Step 8, as we align what we know with what we do, is to use action strategies suitable for the challenges we face. In our work we have observed three patterns of action used by courageous architects of change:

1. The brave and bold seek new ways of doing things—they are disruptive innovators.
2. The brave and bold identify existing solutions that are not yet widespread—they are positive deviants.
3. The brave and bold involve others in learning and mobilizing for solutions—they are adaptive leaders.

Disruptive Innovators: New Ways of Doing Things. As a pivotal force for change, to disrupt does not mean to break something, but to recognize that something is already broken and needs new ideas and unprecedented innovation: ideas that no one, anywhere, at any time, has thought of before. As efficient problem-solvers, disruptive innovators distinguish themselves by crafting and delivering better ways of achieving a goal, of building a better mousetrap.

Patricia Brandes, former executive director of the Barr Foundation, is a strong proponent of disruption in building social capital and bridging gaps among social change leaders. The secret to forging powerful, authentic connections, Brandes asserts, is disruptive—acts that result in change, collaboration, innovation, and, over time, collective impact.[33]

Disruptors innovate—they do not copy. But they do not disrupt simply for the sake of change or creating commotion. They do it to fill gaps, to do what others can't or won't do. They seek new ideas, approaches, and solutions to persistent challenges. Disruptors look for existing practices that seem to be written in stone but are inefficient, illogical, and wasteful. They offer alternatives with a perceived value greater than any existing realities. Bill Drayton, CEO of Asoka, notes that "social entrepreneurs are not content just to fish or teach how to fish. They will not rest until they have revolutionized the fishing industry."[34]

Disruption doesn't necessarily require big, complicated solutions or ideas. Many of the best examples are simple and straightforward. Kathy Gallo illustrates how she became a disruptive innovator in her position as a leader of a regional partnership and distributor of grants in her state. When the funding stream was cut, the partnership faced a crisis, which, if handled poorly, could significantly impact the programmatic and economic needs of the region, and dismantle the already fragile governance process. Proposals began pouring in, the requests for funds outnumbered the available funds, and no one was willing to withdraw their requests. Kathy remembers: "The process utilized by the members included heavy lobbying by each individual partner for their specific needs, and not those of the partnership as a whole."

Kathy recognized obstacles: The partners were not collaborative enough, and getting people to change would not be easy. She made a choice. She took all submitted proposals, "wrote each topic down on a separate sheet of paper, brought them to the meeting, and taped them up all around the room. I opened the door and said, 'How do you feel about looking at it from a topical perspective (what the region needs) rather than from an individual agency perspective?'"

Kathy described the new system as "amazing. When it flushed out, every agency had a role to play." And notably, the innovative system laid the groundwork for a stronger, more collaborative governance process, and facilitated a more trusting and respectful environment among regional partners. Kathy disrupted a system that was no longer working for the current situation. Her resourcefulness and creativity, coupled with her courage to interrupt a broken system, resulted in better outcomes.

The effectiveness of a disruption requires hindsight, like Kathy's reflections. After we implement our innovations, we should look back to assess the impact of our disruptions.

Positive Deviants: Maximizing Existing Solutions. Positive deviance grows from the idea that certain people have uncommon strategies that enable them to achieve success when others cannot. These people's uncommon strategies and behaviors empower them to outperform their peers, even though both groups have (or lack) similar resources. These people are positive deviants, and we are wise to pay attention to their methods and actions.

Richard Pascale, Jerry Sternin, and Monique Sternin, co-authors of *The Power of Positive Deviance*,[35] acknowledge that positive deviance sounds oxymoronic, yet when problems seem absolutely intractable and resistant, people come forward to succeed while others continue to fail. Let's flip our point of view and look at these "deviants" as bright, groundbreaking, and positive—even mainstream in the long run.

The *Power of Positive Deviance* cites three key principles:

- Positive deviants emphasize the transference of behavior, not knowledge. They encourage architects of change to "act your way into a new way of thinking instead of thinking your way into a new way of acting."[36]
- Positive deviants emphasize the relational (people), not the technical (facts, strategies, or policies). The focus is on leveraging formal and informal networks.
- Innovations and solutions come from the "hidden wisdom" within the community.[37] The community's members, not external experts or authorities, generate solutions. Lao-Tzu put it best: "Learn from the people. Plan with the people. Begin with what they have. Build on what they know. Of the best leaders, when the task is accomplished, the people all remark, 'we have done it ourselves.'"[38]

Distressed, educators in Lakeview, Ohio, had a growing number of children who showed up for kindergarten "not ready." Their region of Ohio has high levels of poverty, unemployment, and children who have had no preschool experience, and high rates of kindergarten retention. Aware that the knowledge base provides scant evidence on the benefits of retention, and that additional resources targeted to this issue did not exist, Scott Taylor, Mary Fran Jones, and Mary Lou Bristol asked themselves: What can we do for children and families now and for the rest of the school year to accelerate their success? What could we offer over the summer? What can we do in 1st grade to support children who otherwise would have been retained?

These Ohio leaders drew upon their collective resources to start a summer program that included children with no preschool experience and those who might need a "bit of a refresher." In addition to hands-on experiences, children learned the daily routines of kindergarten such as riding the school bus or eating in the cafeteria. The community strongly embraced this program, and Lakeview beat the odds by creating success experiences for young children.

Adaptive Leadership: Mobilizing People for Solutions. Ron Heifetz defines Adaptive Leadership™ in his classic book, *Leadership Without Easy Answers,* as a set of learned strategies and practices that can help people and groups to tackle tough problems, to thrive in complex, competitive, and challenging environments.[39] The five questions that follow (drawn extensively from the work of Ron Heifetz and his colleagues) help identify when adaptive leadership may be useful:[40]

1. Do you already know the solutions? If so, you have a technical challenge, not an adaptive challenge.
2. Does the problem require new ideas, habits, or behaviors? Situations requiring adaptive leadership demand responses outside of our comfort zone and knowledge base.
3. Do you need to make fundamental choices? Adaptive work involves conflicting values and calls for painful trade-offs, difficult debate, and, potentially, the loss of historically cherished beliefs.
4. Will sustainable change take time to achieve? If your challenge is truly an adaptive one, you must generate engagement through relationships, and relationships take time.

5. Could an effective or charismatic leader make the change? Adaptive challenges require you to catalyze leadership as a collective activity involving many individuals in varied positions with diverse points of contact. Reflecting on this idea, in a CAYL focus group a participant stated: "The role of charismatic leader doesn't provide enough value for the community, because that role is focused on one person—and one person is not enough."

Adaptive leaders use three primary strategies: First: *Focus attention* by building awareness of an issue. "Get on the balcony" to see the bigger picture. Second: *Create a learning environment* with constructive dialogue that preserves a collective responsibility for solving problems. Finally: *Manage tensions that are inevitable* in any change process.

These ideas clearly relate to our fieldwide challenges. "You really have to rise above the mudslinging that goes on," CAYL Fellow Marie Enochty advises. "Yes it's a pain, but it comes with the territory and you have to be willing to keep on. That's where the relationships and community is critical. Never let go of the 'big picture.'"

Keeping the big picture in mind while mobilizing others has been a career focus for Jeri Robinson, a CAYL Fellow and a leader in designing spaces for very young children in museums.

I began working with Boston Children's Museum in the early 1970s. Our audience back then was really 6- to 12-year-olds. There were always lots of siblings in backpacks, but because there was nothing for them to see or do, when they became fussy, the family would leave. So we added programming for the younger children while continuing to accommodate the older ones. Nationally, it was the late 1980s and early 1990s that Children's Museums started discovering early childhood . . . I built allies to start mobilizing people in Head Start and preschools. We worked with families to emphasize the importance of playing with your children. There was a shift from the child focus to the family engagement focus. Now, all over the country you can find these programs in museums, but also in places like airports and prisons.

As an adaptive leader, Jeri shares her lessons learned:

You have to sit at the table and listen just as much as you peddle your wares to find ways of inviting people to you. There was no model for this so we could try out and revise things to become more and more responsive to the needs out there. We could be experimental and thoughtful about issues of "public parenting."

THEORIES ABOUT EVOLUTIONARY BIOLOGY AND LEADERSHIP

Heifetz and his colleagues indicate that adaptive leadership ideas stem from efforts to understand in practical ways the relationship among leadership, adaptation, systems, and change, but also have deep roots in evolutionary biology. Our human ancestors lived in small bands that developed ever-increasing sophistication. Through evolutionary change, they internalized the wisdom of elders, developed cultures with self-sustaining norms, and expanded their communities to a point where they required governing bodies. The human process of adaptation to new possibilities and challenges has continued throughout history, with the growth and variation in scope, structure, governance, strategy, and coordination of political and commercial enterprise; so has the evolution in understanding the practice of managing those processes, including the concept of adaptive leadership. Successful adaption has three characteristics: (1) it preserves the DNA essential for the species' continued survival (what are our norms, values, and purpose?); (2) it discards (reregulates or rearranges) the DNA that no longer serves the species' current needs (how can we anchor change in the best of our wisdom and know-how?); and (3) it creates DNA arrangements that give the species the ability to flourish in new ways and in more challenging environments (change takes time and experimentation). Successful adaptations enable a living system to take the best from its history into the future.[41]

Act with Character and Strategy: Be Architects of Change

Positive deviants, disruptive innovators, and adaptive leaders share the same DNA. They are discerning about the present situation—their current realities. They welcome a fresh sense of collaboration, valuing inclusion over hierarchy. They have expert communication skills and the capacity to welcome and manage complexity. Above all, they are willing to act. These approaches to action respect and celebrate the lived wisdom of people in our profession; they enable underdogs like David—like us—to admit our weaknesses, choose unconventional strategies, and use tools we already know well. They reflect what Peter Senge describes as, "the capacity of a human community to shape its future, to sustain significant change."[42]

Disruptive innovators, positive deviants, and adaptive leaders share the qualities of courage, commitment, and competence. They do not charge blindly into the fray. Change can originate within any one of us, as Senge spells out in *The Necessary Revolution*. Innovators innovate because they feel passion about something. Innovators focus on the big picture, moving beyond short-term perspectives. Leaders know how to connect with lots of people and across established or historical boundaries. Leaders avoid the negativity that tends to pervade the issues in the early education field.[43]

As we speak of leadership, we should not be afraid of the word *power*. Adam Kahane in *Power and Love* suggests that we should not seek power over others but power to lead others to achieve beneficial outcomes. Grand aspirations and good intentions are not enough; leaders can't simply sit by waiting for a pat on the shoulder.[44] Sometimes leaders need to step forward and authorize themselves in the face of resistance, apathy, or the absence of a mandate from others. They trust in winning the backing of others by convincing, not bullying, them. Richard Searle writes:

> Sometimes the leader herself generates apathy, resistance, and ambivalence about a mandate—telling herself all the reasons why she is not the one to act, why this is not her time to act, why it is far too risky. Those who can authorize themselves to lead in the face of their own disempowering identity and judgments are most powerful. Each of us needs to find that quiet place inside ourselves where we can go when this sort of personal courage is called for.[45]

Marianne Williamson describes perhaps our deepest fear when deciding whether to be brave and bold—to act:

> Our deepest fear is not that we are inadequate. Our deepest fear is that we are powerful beyond measure. It is our light, not our darkness, that

most frightens us. We ask ourselves, who am I to be brilliant, gorgeous, talented, and fabulous? Actually, who are you *not* to be? Playing small does not serve the world. There is nothing enlightened about shrinking so that other people won't feel insecure around you. We are all meant to shine, as children do.[46]

Five Smooth Stones

1. *Deviation, Disruption, Adaptation.* Our cloth sack holds the willingness for, as well as the tools of, action that can make life better for children, for families, and for ourselves. We should be flexible and creative in the ways we choose to act.
2. *Courage, Commitment, Competence.* Above all of the stones in our cloth sack, matters of character are perhaps the most important. Walking with integrity matters greatly as we strive to teach responsibly and be agents of social change.
3. *Reconciliation.* Recognize that we *all* make mistakes: Mistakes in judgment, in practice, in words, in thought, in fact. But we also have many opportunities for making adjustments, modifications, amendments, alternations, and revisions, which can correct, improve, and *reconcile* our situation. The stone of reconciliation is in our cloth sack and within our power to use as a cornerstone of our character whenever the occasion warrants.
4. *Principles.* Principles abound in the field of early care and education. There are principles of child development, principles of developmentally appropriate practice, principles of curriculum and assessment, and ethical principles for our profession. These principles have substance, and we should take them seriously. Use them to up our game in our day-to-day interactions with coworkers, supervisors, children, and families. Making concerted efforts for our work lives to be governed by these principles is a must.
5. *Aha! moments.* Most of us have experienced one or more aha! moments of wonderful alignment when our convictions are tested and proven to prevail. Conversely, we may have experienced an aha! moment when we recognized that our thinking or action was in error. Learn from these moments—and do something with our new insights.

Reflect on Becoming an Architect of Change
What Would **You** Do?

1. Think of a situation where you or someone you know has been rebuked or criticized. What did you learn from that situation?

2. Reflect on a time you experienced an aha! moment. What did you do once you experienced this epiphany? What do you wish you had done differently?

3. Use the chart below to think about your leadership style, using examples from any part of your life (your examples do not have to be limited to education).

Personal Quality	Describe the Situation	What Were the Outcomes of the Action?	What Did You Learn from This Experience?
Disruptive Innovator			
Positive Deviant			
Adaptive Leader			

4. Rank your commitment, competence, and courage to act for your children and/or for early educators. How might you become stronger in these areas?

Personal Quality	Rank on a 1 (Low) to 5 (High) Scale	Steps You Can Take to Strengthen This Quality	What You Intend to Do Next
Commitment			
Competence			
Courage			

Where We Are So Far

In just three steps, we have taken substantial leaps into the *ACT!* arena, with certainty that we align what we know with what we do, bringing the power of our knowledge and expertise to bear. And we entered the fray with practicality, starting with the everyday challenges that greet us at the door, everyday—challenges that are reasonable in size (at least to begin). Finally, we have built a confidential community and learned to share leadership.

CHAPTER FOUR

ACCELERATE!—
Believe and Achieve
What Would David Do?

Once David defeats Goliath, the story doesn't end. Though he was greatly loved by his people, tremendous obstacles still lay in the road ahead of him. Eventually, however, David, a young shepherd boy, became a treasured and influential king with new and unexpected allies, accelerating power, and popularity.

Chapter 4 will probably be the most challenging part of our journey—a minimarathon, if you will, that includes important steps toward accelerating change. Like David, we recognize that change is a step-by-step process, not an event—a process chronicled in many of the stories throughout this book. Each step sometimes seems risky, and at times standing still (or doing nothing) feels the safest. But like David, we believe in our cause—and we are willing to take the steps to achieve it.

For early educators, there is an accelerating culture of "belief." The alliance of believers is now deeper and wider, and includes business and labor leaders, economists, governors, mayors, and representatives of many faiths. With alliances, greater results for children are possible because of the heightened sense of urgency, a "bias for action,"[1] and a desire to seize today as a historic moment in time. Acceleration requires the development of systems, not a constant flow of isolated new initiatives. Acceleration requires investments in people—the staff who care for and educate young children. Alliances extend our capacity for courageous action, and greater public willingness to invest more in prevention than remediation. Now, let's pick up speed in our pursuit of change.

This chapter introduces three tools for accelerating our quest for change—tools entirely within our control and ability to perfect. *Step 9,*

Focus on What You Want, Not What You Don't Want, sharpens our awareness that it is easy to get distracted from our goals. While we must remain adaptive and flexible to course changes in the path forward, we need clarity of vision to know when we are going off-course and when Goliath is working to distract us.

Step 10, Don't Walk Alone—Gather Your Allies, is an opportunity to open our eyes and minds to the endless possibilities created by linking arms with like-minded people, communities, and initiatives. Nothing builds momentum like strong, trusted alliances.

Finally, *Step 11, Get the Word Out—Document and Communicate Impact,* does the critical work of sharing our stories: the challenges we faced, how we succeeded, how others might succeed, and lessons learned. With a growing emphasis on results, we must be ready to demonstrate our effectiveness in nurturing and teaching young children. For every family newsletter and speaking appearance at a gathering of local businesspeople, we should be ready to tell our story—and tell it well.

THEORY ABOUT RESOURCE MOBILIZATION

In Chapter 4 we seek to accelerate change. Here we are guided by the ideas of *resource mobilization theory*. Developed in the 1970s, the theory seeks to explain the emergence of social movements. Placing resources at the emergence and success of social movements, resource mobilization theory asserts that social movements form when people who share grievances are able to mobilize resources and take action. Resources do not consist solely of financial support, but also involve media communications, allies, and most important for early educators, the time, labor, and solidarity of its members. The acceleration principle of *The New Early Childhood Professional* is "don't walk alone"; this theory emphasizes the value of networks, collective identity, and ongoing relationships. When resource mobilization theory first appeared, it was a breakthrough in the study of social movements because it focused on variables that are sociological rather than psychological. No longer were social movements viewed as irrational, emotion-driven, and disorganized. For the first time, influences from outside social movements, such as support from various organizations or the government, were taken into account.[2]

STEP 9: FOCUS ON WHAT YOU DO WANT, NOT WHAT YOU DON'T WANT

What can **you** do now?

As you're reading Step 9, identify what you want, and focus on those issues that are timely, relevant, and immediately actionable. Practice mindfulness to focus and strengthen your resolve.

You can't depend on your eyes when your imagination is out of focus.

—Mark Twain[3]

As we face our own Goliaths, there is probably an insistent voice inside us saying: *"Just do something!"* And yet we are cautioned: Our path may be unclear ("If you don't know where you're going, any road will get you there").[4] And unwise choices are possible (should David kill the king in his sleep?). It is hard to overestimate the importance of focused forethought about where we are going—about what we want—before we devote our time, energy, and money to a course of action.

Step 9 offers tools to help us focus on what we want. These tools include the ability to cultivate and practice mindfulness and techniques to evaluate whether our ideas and goals are on track. Step 9 also encourages us to take the long view by maintaining focus on the future, as illustrated by the stories of Kitt Cox and Tamara Blake-Canty.

We're Sure You Know What You Don't Want! But Do You Know What You *Do* Want?

How often has your mind drifted off (while watching television, or riding the subway to work, or grabbing a quick lunch in a quiet corner of the center's playground) to a work problem that plagues you? Or a situation in your city's early care and education system that has bothered you for a very long time? Often, in this drifting, we are thinking about what's wrong, what we want to stop, and what we do not want to happen.

As CAYL participants come together for their year of Fellowship, they spend 3 to 6 months articulating what they want to achieve. This comes as a surprise to many who imagine that creative and highly motivated Fellows already know what they want to do. This is certainly true to a point. Fellows do come to the table fired up about a host of issues: *We want more men in the field! We want better compensation and working conditions! We want respect for family child care! We want home languages to be appreciated! We want all children to have high-quality developmentally appropriate culturally sensitive early care and education! We can't believe* that *policy actually exists—we want to change it!* All of these are excellent starting points—but starting points only.

Sometimes, our advocates get stuck at the starting points. Endless rounds of sharing ideas and experiences can be important, but sharing alone often does not lead to change. Conversations too frequently move in the direction of fear, worry, frustration, anxiety, and other disempowering thoughts, and our focus moves quickly to what we do not want. Sometimes we prefer to talk more about our horrifying day and our Goliath-size problems than how lovely a day would be without them.

When we think about the money we don't have for books and materials, our low compensation, the advanced training we don't have, the playground we can't afford, and the sacrifices we have to make, we're thinking about what we *don't* want. When we think about children on waitlists, who arrive at our programs hungry, or who have no access to early learning programs at all, we're thinking about what we *don't* want. And when we are thinking that some view us as babysitters, that we can't afford to go back to college, or the lack of time we have to be innovative, we are preoccupied with what we *don't* want.

Articulating what's wrong over and over again, even if it's in our minds, doesn't lead to solutions or change. In fact, if voiced loud and often enough, focusing on what we don't want can result in us being labeled whiners, complainers, and people who are not to be taken seriously—thereby weakening the effectiveness of our message and eroding support for the very thing that is important to us.

When we find ourselves thinking or speaking in the negative— what we don't want—we should *stop*. Instead, let's ask ourselves: "What can we say or do that will help this situation? What is a solution to our problem?" We must look inside ourselves—and keep our eyes on the prize. Moving away from thoughts of intimidation, negation, and isolation, the step before us now is a tall one: devoting time and energy toward things we *do* want, not what we *don't* want.

What, exactly, do we want? We do want to thrive—authentically—and not just be chameleons. We want to figure out how to actualize our dreams. *But how?*

Focus on What You *Do* Want!

If we were crystal-clear about what we want, we would give ourselves the permission and strength to imagine new possibilities—to generate ideas to realize what truly matters to us. When we visualize the world we want, we get and give so much more: we open the door to our greatest awareness and creative ideas. Goals become clearer. We make better decisions. Others begin to perceive the calm sense of purpose that keeps us moving proactively. We inspire others and ourselves.

To focus on what we really do want we suggest three strategies: practice mindfulness, ask critical questions, and take the long view.

Practice Mindfulness to Realize Your Focus. Jeremy Hunter of the Drucker School of Management teaches his students that "paying attention to what's happening in the present moment is essential to becoming an effective leader. Good decision-making often comes down to mustering focus, clarity, and calm."[5]

As early educators practicing mindfulness, we pay attention to what is happening in our field. We are aware of the emotions and reactions of both ourselves and others, and prepare to react more skillfully in any situation. Awareness helps reduce stress, but most important, it gives us the ability to step out of whatever reaction we're having—which is usually habitual or automatic. We can focus on what we do want.

Practicing mindfulness has been touted as a big "game-changer" because it can help organizations, groups, and individuals to thrive despite challenging circumstances. When challenged by Goliath, we may unconsciously trigger parts of the brain that give rise to fear and anger. Do not give in to worry. Do not give in to doubt. Do not give in to temporary circumstances. Do not allow our challenges to overwhelm us. When we cultivate mindfulness and calm, we're better equipped to engage the parts of the brain that can respond to everyday challenges, form community, and share leadership. Hunter adopts the phrase "the impartial spectator,"[6] coined by the renowned Adam Smith[7] to describe this ability to see ourselves in a dispassionate and clear way.

Ask Critical Questions

A CAYL Fellowship can be a truly cathartic experience, we have learned over time. *Finally, we are in a room with other deeply passionate colleagues who get it!* In initial gatherings, Fellows almost instinctively start to shrug off the weight of Goliath—this is a necessary step that must happen before we feel creatively free. But then the thought emerges: *What do we do now?* Fortunately, ideas abound.

Being architects of change requires attention to the circumstances that surround us. What do we actually know about the status of men in the field, home languages, or family child care in our communities? Can we name a concrete policy, program, or action as the focus of our attention? What can we do differently? Is our solution timely, relevant, and immediately actionable?

This last question becomes a guiding standard—a critical question—as Fellows weigh strategies and solutions. This question demands, finally, that we start to transform grand Goliaths (poverty, race, or curriculum, for instance) into smaller, doable, serial steps that would benefit from our presence and action (Raul didn't have breakfast this morning; our lunch program doesn't have enough fresh fruits and vegetables; our summer food program for kids needs more public funding).

Is Our Solution Timely? Timeliness means that an issue or activity is occurring at a suitable or opportune moment; a mistimed event can happen either too soon or too late.

Consider the case of some Boston elementary school principals who discovered, after acting on a perception, that kindergarten was the most tested grade level in the entire school system. Feeling safety in numbers, they wrote a position paper heavily informed by the knowledge base about developmentally appropriate assessment, and offered an alternate plan with concrete suggestions for change. They perceived a timely issue, addressed it quickly and thoroughly, and were successful in implementing change in time for future testing cycles.[8]

Is Our Solution Relevant? Relevance means that a plan, action, document, or opinion has a connection to the topic or issue at hand. Relevance has an even more pressing meaning: Something is relevant if it increases the likelihood of accomplishing a goal. In fact, Goliath often uses seemingly correct but irrelevant information to distract or confuse us from the instructional, program, or policy focus at hand (i.e., my school children's parents did not read to them when they were babies, therefore they cannot read on grade level; we can't change children's pasts, so obsessing about their pasts is irrelevant).

When accelerating change, we often find that connecting the relevance of our actions to our broader local communities becomes an important strategy to help us focus on, and obtain, what we want. Bob Walls explains:

> It's about relationships. You have to go out in the community and build relationships. I joined organizations. I worked with the city council, I worked with command council, and the American Legion. I let them see who I am and let them know that they're important to our school.

Elementary principal Jeff Wolf looked around his community and discovered that a sizeable number of children had no formal preschool experiences prior to entering kindergarten—an issue relevant to the success of the elementary school he led. He realized he needed to spend more time on that problem:

> It was like something hit me over the head and said, "Why aren't you paying more attention to this?" So I made some very simple goals for myself. First, I wanted a Saturday morning where I invite parents of preschoolers who have no contact with the school. I sent a letter to every parent and I got a terrific response; they were very excited. That was my first outreach to these parents.

Jeff chose a relevant action in response to his immediate need to know the parents of his future pupils better.

Community outreach was also a part of Cheryl Kirk's efforts to support local children. Cheryl became concerned about the multiple transitions children in her kindergarten and local preschool programs were making on a daily basis as they were shuffled around from program to program. So she began coordinating with local preschool and child-care programs to arrange fewer and better transitions for young children in her district. Cheryl also arranged a way to ensure that kindergarteners in her building (who were enrolled in a half-day program) would be provided a full day of learning, in partnership with an external community program that joined the team.

Is Our Solution Immediately Actionable? Since CAYL Fellowships last 1 year or less, CAYL facilitates a process that teaches Fellows how to create change—a process that they can then use for the rest of their careers. The CAYL Institute encourages Fellows to select problems that are immediately actionable to heighten their potential for success as they practice the process. Ending childhood hunger is an admirable goal—but for one Fellow, or a small group of Fellows, that's a daunting, let's say impossible, goal in the context in which we're working. Kitt Cox's story illustrates how to take immediate action toward a big goal.

Kitt speaks passionately about his experiences as a man working in child care. He entered the field young, with a passion to teach, and believes that more men would enter the field if there were stronger systems to invite, mentor, and encourage them to do so. "People are suspicious about men who want to be around children as a career." He adds:

> They assume we are somewhere between incompetent and abusive, and everything in between. But there's a flip side to it. I get so many more kudos from parents compared to the women I work with in the infant room. They were so sick of it after a while. It was a running joke at the center. The only guy that applies gets the job, and everyone thinks he hung the moon.

Kitt wants more men to be in the field *right now* (not immediately actionable!). Using collaborative networks like Men Teach, Kitt works to achieve that vision as a long-term goal. What else could he do that would be timely, relevant, and immediately actionable? Kitt and his cohort of Fellows (Just Holm, Rolland Janairo, Theresa Jordan, and Nida Wright) discovered that there were no available data in Massachusetts about the gender of people working in the field. An immediately actionable solution? The team successfully gathered state administrative support to start collecting workforce data by gender, and spread the word about the need for more men in the field through a widely distributed policy brief.[9]

Take the Long View: Kitt and Tamara

We focus on what is timely, relevant, and immediately actionable as a means to teach Fellows a process of change, and to facilitate a successful experience. From there we encourage Fellows to take the long view: We are running in a marathon, not a sprint. We encourage a future focus ("plant the seeds today that you want to harvest tomorrow"). If we want to implement change and progress that are genuinely sustainable and positive, we must take the time to allow our plans to come to fruition. Kitt Cox and Tamara Blake-Canty illustrate this point.

Kitt works overtime to create circumstances in which an idea can become actionable. "We got shot down when trying to improve standards in 2006, but I see now that our initial attempt was probably a catalyst for improvements in standards later on." Kitt elaborates:

> We worked for almost a year drafting standards and trying to get the state to adopt them for infants and toddlers in child care. We took them to the Secretary and we were pretty much minimized and negated. They practically patted us on the head. It was insulting. But we didn't take it personally, and we sure as hell didn't stop. We networked more enthusiastically and came at it from a few more directions and involved folks that could be more influential with the Secretary. Three or four years later, it happened.

Currently, Kitt and his coworkers are working to include post-partum depression screening for mothers as part of well-child checks. They are mapping resources through a system of family networks, engaging pediatricians in the issue, and using a cross-state strategy to strengthen their forces. Kitt says, "I can see the momentum building."

Working toward timely, relevant, and immediately actionable goals does not always mean working to influence external forces. Sometimes the change must occur within.

Tamara Blake-Canty became a principal of an elementary school with an early childhood program admittedly "knowing nothing" about early childhood. Initially, she imposed the same methodologies used in the upper elementary grades, watered down for young children. But she quickly discovered by joining a network of educators that an early childhood lens provides a powerful launching point from which an entire school, and its faculty, could be transformed. As she learned about early childhood development, visited other programs and classrooms, and developed an understanding of NAEYC Accreditation standards, Tamara experienced a metamorphosis.

Her transformation included rigor but, more essentially, a solid developmentally appropriate foundation, strong social guidance, child-centered benchmarks, and observational assessments for young learners. The greatest impact came when she changed her school's culture and approach to family engagement, treating families less as outside supporters of their child's learning and more as cofacilitators in the process. She explains:

> I have a better understanding of early childhood now. I know that the centers where children are engaged are not just random; they are purposeful and instructionally driven. And they are connected to curriculum.

Tamara practically beams with the power of the knowledge she has gained, and the strategies being implemented:

> The key component of how children learn is that it has to be hands-on. With the little ones, you can't expect them to sit on the rug for 20 minutes, as the older children may be able to. It's got to be center [play] based. And to be quite honest, I changed my upper elementary because of what is going on in the lower elementary. If you look in the early childhood classroom, there's a lot of center work. Once the children got to 3rd grade there were no centers; the kids were bored. And we were losing them. So we actually started implementing centers in Grades 3, 4, and 5. It's working out very well. The teachers love it. The kids love it.

More globally, a sea change in the school community's perspective on early education has occurred. "Early childhood was looked at as day care. I would hear, 'Teachers? They're not really teachers. They're not teaching down there.' And so we've learned, with the help of the early childhood teachers, to really change the culture."

The transformation has been felt personally as well, Tamara says. "As for myself and other upper-grade teachers, now we go back to the early childhood teachers to say, 'Hey, you know, I have a child who's not doing such and such, can you give me some suggestions?'"

Tamara practiced mindfulness and focus on what she wanted to achieve. She deconstructed the whole into small, doable, serial steps. One doesn't have to be perfect at the first step. In fact, trying to be perfect is a great way to become frustrated (as Voltaire cautioned us, "The best is the enemy of the good"). Just identify and stay focused on what you do want!

Stay Focused on What You *Do* Want!

Success typically comes in small incremental steps. We rarely have dramatic immediate breakthroughs. Yet even small victories can create positive feelings. With one courageously taken step, we may find opportunities to invite new people or organizations into our lives or new insights into our minds. Often one cannot recognize these new partners or ideas when seen through the lens of what we don't want.

As we take these key steps, we accept that there will be days of discouragement and fatigue and plan for this. Think about how we might shift our focus or set our sights on a new goal when the current goal is, for now, unattainable. Set down some expected, measurable milestones to know whether we're staying on the right track. We put together a Plan B and tuck it into our rough sack of stones as another tool to draw upon when the time is right. At every step, we do a "mind check" to confirm that we have a clear idea of what we're doing and a clear vision of what the change will look like when it occurs.

FIVE SMOOTH STONES

1. *Focus*. Focus on what we want. Concentrate our attention and energy on the ideas about which we are seeking solutions. Goliath distracts—and distractions abound!
2. *Solutions*. Almost every "don't want" situation can be restated as a "do want," which can point the way to solutions. No idea is too zany to consider. We don't let the best idea be the enemy of the good.
3. *Desire*. Focus is best achieved when our intentions are strongly desired, anticipated, and expected. Desire is the fire that energizes us and keeps burning through disappointments and delays.
4. *Clarity*. David had clarity. He knew exactly what results he wanted to achieve and when he wanted to achieve them. *Exactly*. Not a guess or an approximation. As Stephen Covey would say, David began with the end in mind.[10] His intentions were established. Without clarity, Goliathan forces can easily manipulate us. When we are working together "on purpose," many of our challenges become solvable, and we can achieve amazing results. So let's write down our goals and the time frame in which we intend to achieve them. Specify how our success will be measured. Set our vision and take the first steps.

5. *Perseverance.* Among the many legends about Winston Churchill is the belief that he said, "Never, never, never give up." Keep a steady persistence in our course of action, even though there may be difficulties and obstacles, and at times we may feel discouraged. Another legend who attributes his success to his failures is Michael Jordan, one of the best basketball players of all time. "I've missed more than 9,000 shots in my career. I've lost almost 300 games. Twenty-six times, I've been trusted to take the game winning shot and missed. I've failed over and over and over again in my life. And that is why I succeed."[11] Hold tight to that stone of hope. Persevere!

REFLECT ON BECOMING AN ARCHITECT OF CHANGE
WHAT WOULD **YOU** DO?

ACCELERATE! Believe and Achieve   Step 9: Focus on What You Do Want, Not What You Don't Want

Maintaining proper focus means becoming adept at visualization and mindfulness. Through single-mindedness and concentrated intention, we will prevail as architects of change.

1. How can you use the concept of mindfulness to maintain your focus?

2. List three to five responses to the question: What do I as an early educator ultimately want? Then, brainstorm as many solutions as possible.

3. Hone in on a few of your solutions. Which solutions are most: Timely? Relevant? Immediately actionable?

4. What are your first next steps to address one possible solution?

5. Today is the day to:

STEP 10: DON'T WALK ALONE—GATHER YOUR ALLIES

What can **you** do now?

As you read through Step 10, think about how you will identify and engage the allies you will need to make the changes you have in mind.

> May we be fearless . . . from friends and enemies . . . from known and unknown . . . from night and day . . . may all the directions be our allies.
>
> —Atharva Veda[12]

Early educators, our children, and their families need powerful friends. No matter how reasonable or clear our goals, we are much more likely to accomplish them with strong, strategic alliances both inside and outside of our early childhood communities.

Why Are Allies Important?

Early care and education is a matter of public import and public policy—a democratic construct—that calls for many minds and many hands working together. Allies bring strength in numbers, enhancing our capacity to face asymmetrical conflict.

Allies add voice and credibility to audiences outside of our reach. An ally can drop a word of encouragement at the right time, and in the right ear. Our work accelerates when we have allies who give us more traction with people and in places that we could not enter alone. Allies make it possible to build public buy-in that we could not possibly achieve on our own.

An ally can offer material assistance, unique skills, access to technology, or new communication channels. Allies possess expertise and add complementary value to our knowledge base—they boost our know-how. We will bounce back more quickly from setbacks or failure by accessing the mix of talent and ability available from many sources.

Our allies join with us for many reasons. Among these reasons is their understanding that injustice for children and for early educators should not be tolerated. Allies are part of the adult community that loves children and respects childhood. And often, they not only share our ideals, they live them because they are parents, families, friends, and cultural or spiritual leaders for children.

Some of our allies act because they genuinely respect our field. And, yes, some of our allies act out of their own self-interests. They buy or sell products and services to children, families, or our industry. Nevertheless, we need allies, as they need us, so let's be pragmatic and appreciate whatever positive contribution an ally has to offer.

Ultimately, the sustainability of our change efforts requires our alignment with, or transformation of, the society in which we function. Our progress requires the consent of widely diverse groups of individuals and organizations. We must exercise greater fieldwide leadership if we are to be strong partners with our allies. In addition, it is a mistake—sometimes a fatal one—when we take the position that we can do it all ourselves, or feel free to ignore those who have an interest in our work, for whatever reason. We must take all of our societal relationships seriously and implement strategies to inform and share leadership with them. In this way, we maximize the potential to survive and thrive despite asymmetrical challenges.

Who Are Potential Allies?

The ideas and opportunities to build alliances seem endless, even in the most resource-strapped communities. In his past assignment in a rural community, Principal Matthew Bowen, now superintendent of Campbell City Schools, gathers allies from as many sources as he can:

> We have a "Success by Six Program," sponsored by the
> United Way, to offer a transition for students from preschool
> to kindergartners; early student needs are revealed . . . and
> in September we are able to immediately respond to those
> identified needs. Our teachers no longer experience those
> awkward first weeks of kindergarten where we're still
> learning personalities, behaviors, and abilities of the children.
> Additionally, a partnership with Walsh University was created
> to support integrated technology . . . and all of our teachers
> have received college credit at no cost where they integrated
> technology in the classroom. . . . Kent State-Salem hosted their
> educational psychology class from the elementary building

for aspiring teachers. We've done a lot with engaging our community and reaching out to our local preschools. It takes a variety of partnerships to make a difference for all students in the building.

Every savvy educator knows that families can be amazing sources of useful activism and advocacy. Our first or most immediate allies will most likely come through the families we serve. Creating "good vibrations" with families and communities helps to build goodwill and promote understanding of our work. Some of the success of Haynes Early Learning Center can be attributed to welcoming families as partners and allies, as Valerie Gumes explains:

> I often call on the good graces of people. We continually foster a climate of open communication, promoting shared leadership, safety and security, respect for every individual, and the idea that the school is the center of the community. Supporting parents in becoming more knowledgeable about their child's learning is a continuous process. We encourage parents to become meaningfully involved in the school through curriculum-based workshops and information-sharing.

Matthew Bowen also recognizes the power of parent and community allies:

> We increased kindergarten parent participation by about 80% over what it was 2 years ago. After we got the parents more involved, we said, "You know what? We need to do some more with our preschool directors and our preschool teachers." So, we reached out to them, and we do book studies with them. We have regular conversations with them. We share, with parent permission, some information about students that are coming into our kindergarten program. That has evolved into an all-day kindergarten event, which is a transition day. This really alleviates a lot of the stress not only for the children, but also for the parents. It just makes for a wonderful day, and we have received a lot of praise."

In addition to families, allies include professionals with whom we've worked for years, as well as business, academic, or political leaders. Use your relationships with libraries, museums, and recreation programs to build awareness and commitment to the causes you care about. Whenever possible, bring community leaders to your physical spaces; sponsor annual or semi-annual events in your facilities to celebrate holidays, back to school, literacy, Earth Day, summer day planning, or any idea you can imagine. Remember the four Fs—families, friends, food, and fun.

CAYL Fellow Dianne Bruce, executive director of Edward Street Child Services in Worcester, MA, also understands the power of effective alliances, and she used them to create an annual communitywide Day of Play. With a wide range of allies and financial sponsors, thousands of local residents from many walks of life attend, strengthening their awareness and commitment to the early years. Diane found that new alliances emerged from those she had already built.

As Dianne discovered, the business community can also be powerful allies for us. The vendors who supply our programs with products, services, and foods are potential natural allies. At the national level, The Committee for Economic Development makes the business case for investing in young children because of the critical role early care and education plays in the national economy. Their report advises business leaders about what they can do to support children from birth to age eight. We can review this information and take it with us when we visit business leaders in our town or city.[13]

In building alliances, we can do something we've never done with people with whom we've never before engaged: consider being a candidate for public office, like CAYL Fellows Marie Enochty or Francia Wisnewski.

When Francia Wisnewski became a mother, she was amazed and inspired by her baby, and wanted to know more about how a child grows and develops. She emigrated from Colombia and, now more than ever, wanted to understand more about the American culture in which she would raise her children. Eventually, Francia became a family child-care provider, nurturing and giving care and support to other families who were new to the culture. Francia deepened her skills and knowledge, creating substantial networks and interwoven connections with other child-care providers. Recognizing the need to build more public will and for high-quality early care and education, following her Fellowship experience, Francia succeeded in a run for public office in 2012, when she was elected to serve on the Greenfield, Massachusetts School Committee. A few weeks before the election,

Francia quipped, "Oh, I'm gonna win . . . the people know what I stand for—children and family and education."

As a seasoned elected official and early educator, Marie Enochty joined the CAYL Fellowship with extensive experience in breaking new ground with potential allies:

> I was elected to my local school committee and served for over 10 years. It started when I recognized that the school committee was not knowledgeable enough about early education in general, and there were issues with practice in our district. On top of that there also wasn't enough community and parent engagement at that level. I felt that by getting ourselves organized we could protect the integrated preschool classrooms in the district from being dismantled.
>
> The decisionmaking almost had a cliquey feeling to it, and there didn't seem like there was enough know-how at the school committee level about what little kids really need and what some of our families were facing. It was so important for the families to be activated and more politically engaged—they're the ones that really made the changes. It just took someone supporting them in seeing that there was a way to make it better and that it was possible if we worked together.
>
> At first my work was all about building relationships with individual people. The school committee folks, parents, some people from the recreation department, and the police department got on board. Because I am an early educator I could provide "technical support" to the families, helping them frame their message so they wouldn't be negated as whiny moms. Once I was on the school committee I could lobby the people I thought were potential allies—just in everyday conversations. Sure, there were barriers and challenges from the start. Let's face it: I'm not exactly a "good ol' boy" so relationship-building was really important. I can't say enough about that—people had to see me as part of their community—their neighbor and friend.
>
> For me it boiled down to my commitment to this field. I really care what happens to our children. I could see that it was a high-stakes situation. Of course there are always some losses and disappointments with this vote or that, or people not really stepping up to the plate when you counted on them. We never let go of the "big picture," which was to preserve the integrated

preschool classrooms in the district. We took the politics and losses in stride as part of the journey—and we never, ever gave up. After a decade of service on the school committee the integrated preschool classrooms are still intact.

If being a public official is not where our passion lies, we can nevertheless achieve first-name relationships with those who hold elected office such as town council representatives, mayors, school committee members, and superintendents. When these people see us coming, they should know who we are and what we're all about. Of course, they might think of us as a potential irritant-on-the-way some days, but if we come to champion first-quality early childhood programs—and others know that——they may line up beside us to exercise their power to help. As a social movement, early care and education must develop and sustain allies from all walks of life. The commitment to young children needs to happen everywhere, in every social and economic circle. Our cause must gain widespread appeal in both opinion polls and active support.

Finally, we must never give up in seeking unlikely allies—mainly those who have been skeptical of our cause in the past. For example, Chrissy Pruitt's expertise was negated by her school's purchasing officer, who refused to process orders for materials that he felt were "for playing" and were not "rigorous" enough for school learning. He had questioned Chrissy's judgment as a new principal for submitting such an order. Even though the district did not provide the right materials for young children right away, over the course of the school year, Chrissy was thoughtful and intentional in maintaining dialogue about developmentally appropriate practice with the purchaser. The following year, the same administrator did not hesitate to order the developmentally appropriate materials on Chrissy's list. Chrissy earned an unexpected ally. And, 3 years later, Chrissy's school district became one of a handful in Massachusetts to offer a free all-day kindergarten program for all children.

Engaging Our Allies

For Chrissy and for many of us, alliance-building is a delicate process that can easily go astray. It takes time and effort and, at times, a willingness to accept not getting everything that we want when we want it. We must use our allies strategically, understanding the asymmetrical dynamics that can occur.

We are mindful of the fact that our allies have agendas of their own and may not agree with us in every situation. The best alliances serve the interests of all parties and bring mutual rewards. Nevertheless, because we are the ones seeking support, we take responsibility to establish clear and appropriate communication. Be available to work at the other's convenience, listen to their perspectives, and work closely to devise strategies and solutions. Invest the time in the relationships that the challenges deserve. When conflict arises, mend fences quickly, and remember that we are seeking alignment, not total agreement.

In her work on strategic alliances, Rosabeth Moss Kanter reminds us that allies work together on many levels. Strategic integration takes place at the highest levels and deals with organizational goals and objectives. Tactical and operational integration allows for project planning and spells out the information, resources, or people needed to accomplish the tasks. And, critically, interpersonal and cultural integration provide opportunities for relationships to develop across organizational boundaries, bringing to bear the communication skills and cultural awareness allies need to bridge their differences.[14]

If we are part of an organization that makes an alliance with another organization or group, consider and select potential partners with intention and care. Finding the right points of alignment and agreement can prevent endless negotiating among allies down the road. Be sure that expectations are clear. Establish appropriate structure and processes to keep things moving forward. Keep the details flexible as circumstances change, and revisit the particulars together with your partners to adjust as necessary. Our goal is to achieve stability and clarity to create conditions for success, not lock everyone into stressful, unrealistic commitments.

Most nonchild-serving organizations that join with us do so in order to engage with a powerful mission—to help make a difference in the world. Figure out how to leverage our work in service of your allies' goals and hopes. In as many ways as possible, keep our allies connected to the "big picture" and meaningful purpose that our work offers.

Keeping an Eye on Relationships!

Whether formal or informal, alliances should be purposeful and add value to our cause. As we develop working relationships with some of our allies, it is important to be mindful of how well our collaborative work is proceeding. Keep in mind that any alliance is dynamic and can be affected by other external and internal factors. Manage the alliance to guarantee momentum and ensure that commitments are met. Again, remember—alignment matters more than total agreement.

Effective communication forms the foundation for a positive alliance. We need to be able to tell our potential allies what we need and listen deeply to what they can provide (and what they themselves need). Put ourselves in our allies' shoes and respect their points of view that may be different from our own. Strategic alliances rely on shared leadership to endure. All parties must be able to talk about what is and isn't working in a safe and supportive environment—a confidential community.

We've all heard the adage "if you want to have a friend, be a friend." Well, the best way to have an ally is to be an ally. Let's throw our support behind our allies and their missions, too. Publicly express backing for our ally's desired direction. Be among the first to verbally offer encouragement and reinforcement for what our ally finds important, when possible. Don't wait to see which direction the rest of the group is heading. Demonstrate professional courage and speak up early.

Ensure that our relationships are mutual, even if there are imbalances in power. While elected officials or business leaders may have more financial or political influence, we have valuable information and networks of our own. An easy and effective way to promote the development of strong working relationships is to make it easy for allies to give us their input—whether or how we act on it is a different matter.

Don't think of allies as those from whom we "get." Whenever you knock on the door of a potential ally, bring a gift: the name and phone number of a new contact who might be useful, news from a just-published early childhood study relevant to your mutual cause, a child's drawing celebrating the vernal equinox, or a favorite cup of coffee or tea. Remember: we can be just as great an asset for them as they are for us!

Our allies are human beings, too, who want to feel connected with us. Make sure our allies know that we value them, and take into consideration their perspectives when making decisions or speaking on behalf of our alliance.

Efforts to build alliances definitely pay off, particular in a state like Massachusetts where statewide leadership development of early educators has been a priority. Webs of alliances accelerate the change process, as Marie Enochty observes:

Over the years I see layers of connections building. All of a sudden, several CAYL Fellows work in the state Department of Early Education and Care. All of a sudden, people we meet at CAYL events see us. Right off, there's better communication, collaboration, networking, and relationships. There are those real connections that just might help you be heard.

Insularity is the enemy of good advocacy and social change. The good news is that we have the ability and opportunity to create positive and productive relationships with a wide range of other people, disciplines, and organizations. We sustain relationships when we make ourselves predictable (i.e., close the gap between promises made and promises realized), and we promote harmony when we take the time to educate potential allies about our work.

"At no time did we fool ourselves into thinking we could accomplish what we have done without the help of others. Cultivating relationships has been key," said Mary Lou Bristol, speaking of her work with Scott Taylor and Mary Fran Jones. Bristol noted, "We really opened up communication with the community, sometimes just to share an ice cream with peer educators from other schools at Dairy Queen."

Bob Walls: Building Allies in All Directions

Bob Walls has used a series of strategic and ongoing communication approaches to build community support for the transformation of his local school, to bring new resources to the school program, and to support early childhood programs. He leverages relationships to generate an ongoing cycle of "buzz" around his once-failing school, creating enormous buy-in that contributes to the children's accelerating success.

First: We observed Bob creating alliances with his internal staff and local families, so that they would become ambassadors of the change he envisioned.

You have to talk about it from all levels. Staff members and people who work for the school are your allies. You have to recognize the cooks, the aides, the custodians, and the librarians. And, it can't be fake. They must feel like they're part of the process. You have to sit with them and have hard conversations about what's best for children. Then, there are families: Our school heavily involves families because it enlists their support doing the same things with children at home that we're doing in school programs. I show parents that they're needed, wanted, and their ideas are important. I allow every parent to have lunch or breakfast with their child, to come into school and see what we're doing. Give us some ideas. You'll get those who "ride the fence," so you have to make them feel important, make them feel that they are part of the family. But you can't stop trying. It's a process we take on each year and build on it.

Second: We observed Bob building bridges and bonds across cultures in new ways. "The composition of children here has been changing and becoming more diverse. But it can take time for diverse populations in schools to get used to one another." He has actively celebrated cultures and respectfully rejected occasional demands that would sustain barriers in this ethnically defined community.

Third: Bob created relationships with a wide range of community partners to bring needed financial and moral support to the school.

We brought in a grant through the Swanson Foundation to provide social services inside the building so kids can get counseling at the school. We brought in antibullying ideas. We expanded our summer program and started a Jump Start program and Success by 6. And we started a Spark Program, aimed at 4-year-olds.

Upon learning that many children in his school were experiencing food insecurity, Bob joined with local community groups and received donations and grant money to initiate a "backpack" program; now, every Friday about 150 children leave school with a backpack full of food to get them through the weekend. He secured a grant to have a dental van come to the school twice a year to provide free treatments for students, and found a partner to implement mental health resources for kids. After sustaining the loss of a summer school program, Bob brought in Neighborhood Ministries to fill the void, which welcomed Campbell Elementary students to join their summer learning program. This program gave many students immensely valuable additional instructional support over the summer, easing their transition into a new grade in the fall.

Bob realized that he could not rely solely on the resources of the school system. To build student and family incentive systems, he drew heavily upon community resources. "I let them see who I am and let them know that they're important to our school. The main thing is you never give up."

FIVE SMOOTH STONES

1. *Relationships.* We are strengthened, supported, guided, encouraged, corrected, and affirmed in our relationships. The ability to build strong, long-lasting relationships is likely to be a key factor in determining whether we will be successful for any length of time. Building relationships with children, families, the business communities, and legislators—all relationships take time and effort to both establish and sustain. We look for opportunities to connect with others in our everyday life, and we are likely to find abundant opportunities.

2. *Expectations.* No matter our current realities, expect great things to happen. Always allow our minds to stay in a place of open positive expectation, not creating any negative conclusion about a particular happening. Avoid negative conclusions and all assumptions. Seeing all events as ultimately leading to a more positive outcome is a powerful way to allow wellness and well-being to constantly flow into our reality.

3. *Reciprocity.* Reciprocity has long been recognized as a critical factor in group life and social interaction. Reciprocity means that we cooperate with others; treat others as they treat us; and give favors to those who cooperate with us.

4. *Construction.* Build, don't destroy. We come to the early childhood space to participate in the construction of lives, and in the development of meaning among children, families, and ourselves.

5. *Power.* With our allies, we are powerful. With our power, we walk humbly, and with determination, to create a better world for children and families. We understand that with great power comes great responsibility! We accept responsibility—therefore we accept power.

Reflect On Becoming an Architect of Change
What Would **You** Do?

Strong and sustainable strategic alliances are powerful. Trust and communication form the foundation for relationships.

1. List some of the allies—individual people or groups—upon whom you currently rely for support.

2. It is critical that you do not walk alone! Who can you identify as potential allies (people or groups), and how will you engage them?

3. What are some of the strengths and challenges you have had (or expect to have) in working with allies?

4. Disagreement is an inevitable part of growth and change. We have to be able to manage our disagreements effectively. What are some of the techniques you've used to recognize disharmony with your allies and work out legitimate conflicts?

STEP 11: GET THE WORD OUT—
DOCUMENT AND COMMUNICATE IMPACT

What can **you** do now?

As you read through Step 11, consider the importance of creating local narratives to record your successes and achievements. Document the day-to-day techniques you use to communicate your lessons learned with your families, colleagues, allies, and the world at large.

> The single biggest problem in communication is the illusion that it has taken place.
>
> —George Bernard Shaw[15]

The story of David and Goliath is just that—a story—told over and over throughout the centuries and resonating with one generation after the next because of its core connection to the human experience. The very existence of the David and Goliath story, shared through a variety of mediums, speaks to the importance of recording important events—achievements, historical events, fables, myths, facts, fictions—to provide a framework for moving forward and for accelerating change.

The Illusion

More often than not, many assume that "everybody knows" how important the early years are. After all, this issue was a cover story in *Time* magazine's February 3, 1997, issue, and has experienced huge public visibility.[16] This common perspective is only partly true. Does the average person really know what exactly goes on in a high-quality program? Why is per-child funding declining even as "visibility" increases?[17] Why have there not been dramatic changes in compensation equity for our workforce? Why don't we have stronger fieldwide unity and professionalism? More needs to be said.

Let us not fall under the illusion that the communication work is done. Our efforts must always be multidimensional and evergreen— and we must keep them straightforward and simple.

It's Not a Done Deal: Communication Still Matters

Telling stories matters. Our stories are being—and will continue to be—told by ourselves and by others. Bringing intentionality to our communication strategies is one means by which we actively participate in shaping the narrative about our work. With or without our involvement, our collective narrative is created by what we actually say and what we actually do—our reputation.

In the past decade, many early childhood groups have spent a great deal of time thinking about the best ways to communicate the value of early care and education to the public. The narrative that we have been putting forward, as a result of public opinion polls and other strategies, is a simple one: Early education (emphasis on education, not care) matters for school reform, for closing achievement gaps, and for our national economy. And this message, in our view, has been effective in raising both public visibility and willingness to invest in the early care and education field, especially for the 4-year-old. Success!

But, that is not the whole story. There are missing elements to the narrative. No one is born at age 4. And, even for the 4-year-old, both funding and implementation matter. More, our knowledge base points to the value of comprehensive services, not just preschool education, as key to child outcomes.[18] Even getting the public to acknowledge the early years remains a challenge: A 2010 study conducted by Frameworks[19] reported that people viewed education through a very narrow lens centered in their experience with individual classrooms or schools, and did not see it as a "system" at all. According to the study, interviewees focused immediately and exclusively on the K–12 years, even when prompted to discuss pre-K or higher education.

In this situation, a "credibility gap" for early educators could be imminent. When reflecting on "the big picture," and our current realities, speaking with integrity can be complicated—and it is difficult to fake "chameleon-style."

Frustrated, many early educators fear that politicians and business leaders are moving the early education agenda without us. People in those roles can be great allies of early educators. However, the extent to which they consider our input matters. Friends and allies alike must be encouraged to listen carefully to early educators and to respect our voices and experiences. Without question, these allies play a vital role—and one of those roles is to support our own voices, affording us space to do our own work without sidelining us as props in our own profession.

Bring the Message Home: Local News Is Good News

There are numerous national organizations that will, as part of their mission, continue to spread the word about the big picture for early care and education. They will hire expert consultants, conduct focus groups, and interact with the national press corps. This work is of extraordinary value, but it is not all that must be done. Local efforts can learn from and align with these national efforts. For example, The Annie B. Casey Foundation[20] study focused on identifying those communication strategies that might prove to be most effective or successful in influencing public policy from the perspectives of media outlets. The lessons learned included building relationships; making information accessible, concise, and concrete; using social media, including locally relevant information; humanizing the story behind the statistic; and framing policy solutions in a local context.

What we do in our local communities to supplement and reinforce the importance of the early years is a critical part of the communication package. Local matters!

Today, we have every oral, print, and digital medium imaginable to tell our tales of striding into asymmetrical conflicts and beating the odds. Still, many of us are ill-prepared to take advantage of the new communication environments. Many early care and education programs are poorly branded and inattentive to communication issues.

We urge everyone to show off your early childhood expertise and work. When your efforts bring results, tell others about it! Be strategic and bold in your efforts to inform people who might not know about the work we are doing (positive gossip is great gossip!). When we speak of our success in our hometowns, we raise the profile of the young children we serve, reiterate the importance of this stage and their lives, and highlight the role of early educators. We have a tremendous opportunity to communicate in a more personal way, and to share our excitement and optimism, our skills and knowledge, and our struggles and accomplishments.

You Have Opportunities to Communicate

There is power in local success. At best, it illustrates what is possible on a national scale. Even as data about early childhood become widely available to the national media, the general public wants to know how early care and education programs may contribute to their neighborhood, town, or state.

Again, cast down your bucket where you are and tell the story that you know. Make it local—real and relevant. Chances are, you have quite a story to tell. The more we see and hear about what our colleagues are doing, not just locally but in other parts of the country, the sooner those stories will blend into a core narrative of our work.

In Step 11, believe in and achieve the role you can play to document and communicate the impact of early care and education rewards. Brian Tracy reminds us that: "Communication is a skill that you can learn. It's like riding a bicycle or typing. If you're willing to work at it, you can rapidly improve the quality of every part of your life."[21] Ask yourself:

- What are we doing that people need to know about?
- How can I give visibility to young children—and to early educators—in my community?
- How can I use data to tell stories?

Maria Paulino: Simple Yet Powerful. In a smart move, CAYL Fellow Maria Paulino, owner of an early care and education program in Fitchburg, Massachusetts, uses Facebook to keep in touch with her community and families. Careful to protect children's identities, she posts frequently about the learning activities and curriculum in her program. The Fitchburg newspaper regularly carries features about the program. Local celebrities and politicians visit often. Maria has given voice to the needs of the children in her community, most of whom are dual-language learners and come from low-income families. She also shows her community what high-quality early learning actually looks like.

Maria has learned that the communication process is circular: Communication engages us as owners of our work, which increases interest and broader participation, which in turn fosters more communication. Effective communication for Maria is an interactive process in which information, knowledge, and skills are exchanged both in person and through media. Many people in Fitchburg chat about Maria's program—even those who have no children or grandchildren in Maria's care. Maria's work has become a matter of community pride.

Bob Walls: Communication as a Strategy for Success. Creating an ongoing cycle of buzz has been an essential element to Bob Walls' success. Bob believes in letting people know when "we met or exceeded our expectations . . . knowing that gives us all a sense of accomplishment, raises morale, and reports to the community how it's all going."

Celebrating the small and big victories, he said, leads to further achievements and lets people know how important they are in the process. In his school, excellence is rewarded and heralded constantly in local press and communication outlets. "The first small victories were student of the month, teacher of the month, staff member of the month, volunteer of the month. Every time a child did something and was 'caught' doing well, we rewarded him or her. We showed teachers the growth in their students."

When kindergarten children meet their goals, they join Bob's Principals Club, where they have pizza together and receive a medal. First- through fourth-graders receive honorary dog tags when they meet certain math goals. And for teachers, "We have banquets twice a year to celebrate and meet academic colleagues in other buildings and beyond our community." At the end of the year, new bicycles are donated to students who have met certain goals. And all of these events are "newsworthy" in Bob's community.

Bob makes an important distinction when celebrating and communicating progress: He emphasizes growth over achievement. "A more conclusive sign of success is to track progress made rather than focus on the end goal, such as a student receiving an A. I want teachers and students to feel proud of the progress they've made," he said, and he uses definitive data to demonstrate progress. "You need to build people up by saying we are winning, we are showing growth, our kids are learning. We may not be getting the highest scores, but we have grown."

Plan to Communicate

An important point to recognize is that both Maria and Bob *plan* to communicate, and to continue on an ongoing basis. Further, Bob's story illustrates the importance of telling stories—memorable stories—as well as making a balance between the "facts" and the "emotions."

Often, we are so busy responding to children and families that at the end of the day, putting together a communications plan can seem like a real (nonpriority) luxury. Please, don't put this task aside. It would be tragic if your long hours of work and dedication each day, and their attendant results, went unknown and unappreciated.

There are no more excuses for not sharing our experiences and stories and lessons learned. In addition to new technologies and social media, many traditional approaches continue to support knowledge generation and transfer. The tools and platforms are endless. At a time when there is so much competition for people's attention, we must all become active and strategic communicators to keep our cause alive.

Opportunities to Reach Out

Below is a partial list of both large and small ways we can bring the good news to our audiences:

- Sharing (or writing) peer-reviewed research literature;
- Participating in seminars, conference talks, abstracts, and poster sessions;
- Writing newspaper articles;
- Appearing on television and radio;
- Giving visual presentations on-site and in the community;
- Writing articles in town newsletters;
- Making appearances and brief speeches at community events;
- Displaying children's work in libraries, grocery stores, or other public places;
- Creating a dedicated website for your program (update it often!); and
- Many, many others, limited only by the imagination.

Ten Tips on Telling Our Stories

Communication matters for us because it helps shape our professional reputation—our credibility. When thinking about the "big picture" of communication in our field, we recommend the following guidelines:

1. *Remember the audience!* Whatever we communicate, we are mindful of our audience and their needs, values, and beliefs. Whatever and whenever we communicate, we *must* fulfill a need of our audience. This may sound counterintuitive—after all, if we're taking the time and effort to communicate, should it not be to meet *our* needs? No. By bringing some new piece of information, or a new way of looking at an old issue, or some value that makes it worth their time to pay attention to our message, we are doing double duty: raising our profile as a valuable community communicator and "expanding messages"

to include others. Every time we "send out" a message, in a letter, online, or in person, we inject something of value for our audience. Don't just share our own content and information over and over, because it will come off as naked self-promotion. Social media space, in particular, can't be social without communicating about others as well. Your audience will appreciate it, and come back to hear from you again.

2. *Always tell the truth.* Transparency is healthy. A new reality of the information age is that transparency is no longer a choice. If we don't offer it to the world, the world will impose it on us. In the age of the Internet, social media, and 24-hour news cycles, it has become virtually impossible to hide our sector differences, our quality lapses—really anything at all. We must assume that virtually everything we do will eventually come to public light. If we can't explain where we are as a field, why we are where we are, what we are going to do about it, and the exciting possibilities for the future, we are in trouble.

3. *Speak with moral authority* on behalf of children and families, grounded in our professional ethics—but don't sound overbearing and judgmental. We must continually demonstrate that our values are aligned with the highest visions of a democratic society. To maximize the chance of fieldwide commitment to these values, we strongly urge active conversations about them that include everyone through conferences, education, and, many opportunities. Remember David facing Goliath, swinging his slingshot in the air over his head as he charged forward? That's the spirit of your communication plan: ready, aggressive, relevant, and innovative.

4. *Be authentic and consistent* in your identity as an early educator, from whatever sector you speak. We want people to recognize and trust us and our distinctive field of study and purpose. We are all early educators. Say so, and repeat as necessary.

5. *Interact with people.* Use two-way communication, not a one-way dissemination of information. Value dialogue and engagement. Offer opportunities for input and participation. Build relationships and use various technologies, including the Internet and social media. People can filter out anything that they do not find interesting or informative, so interact with them like a friend.

6. *Present value to our allies.* Cocreate and work with your allies to evolve our communication plans. When we cocreate with allies, we expand our influence. Make sure our touch points encompass everyone we can possibly reach. Look for opportunities to "piggyback" with other communications efforts, and keep an eye out for the gaps that your outreach can fill. Before launching any kind of outreach initiative, become familiar with what other agencies and organizations are doing in your area. In order to avoid duplication of effort, don't hesitate to borrow a successful strategy from someplace else (with permission, of course), and modify it to suit your children and community.

7. *Value is further increased when we learn to speak the language and address the concerns of other people*—that is, when we know which parts of our story hold value for them, and which do not. *Important note:* Presenting value to our allies does *not* mean that we abandon the parts of our story that are less important to them—but rather that we are attentive to their concerns while maintaining our professional integrity. As a strategy for building a social movement, this makes it easier for people to join us.

8. *Avoid "shrinking messages"* that emphasize what happens to *us* (for example, funding cuts), and instead put out "expanding messages" that emphasize *how the system oppresses other people* (i.e., children are not being well served).Connect the impact of your information to positive value for children, families, and communities—it's even better if it can be something specific to which everyone can relate. Show what really matters to people and look for aspects with which everyone can identify.

9. *Be ready for anything.* Have a "crisis communication" plan even though you hope to never use it. Are you ready for such a communication challenge? What will you say when new studies, such as that in Tennessee,[22] show that preschool investments fade out by 3rd grade? Or, on a more local scale, how would you handle an accident or challenge? Be prepared.

10. *Share data when possible.* When making our case or telling our story, we gather evidence to make the accomplishments of our programs visible. Give the achievements of young children and educators meaning with hard facts. Thoughtfully review our program portfolios or institutional data to pick

the ripest informational "fruit" to boost support for early care and education. Use what we already know about observing and documenting children's learning, program quality, or staff achievements in ways that make these accomplishments visible. Think like a marketer—how can such documentation and evidence be brought to bear against the Goliathan weights in our field?

Five Smooth Stones

1. *Celebrations.* With pride, we take time to notice and reflect on how far we have come. We know how important it is to pause, to acknowledge, and to experience the joy of our efforts. Celebrate! We've earned it.
2. *Connections.* When we share the news on our initiatives and accomplishments, we open the door to new connections. We are always ready to invite others to join the cause for both early educators and for young children!
3. *Extensions.* Today, more than ever, the possibility to extend our reach seems endless. We acquire digital literacy and use all possible means to extend our message.
4. *Creations.* New communication and evaluation methodologies encourage our creativity. We imagine new ways to tell our stories and spread the word.
5. *Voices.* No one person speaks for us; we are many. We prosper when there are multiple and diverse voices.

Reflect on Becoming an Architect of Change
What Would **You** Do?

ACCELERATE! Believe and Achieve   Step 11: Get the Word Out—Document and Communicate Impact

1. What are you doing that could be shared?

2. Make a list of individuals and groups who need to know about what you or others are doing (e.g., family members, politicians, administrators, media, funders, etc.).

3. How would you evaluate the effectiveness of communication strategies you or your program have used (i.e., newspaper articles, social media, public forums, meetings, workshops)?

4. What communication strategies would you be willing to try, or to invest more time doing?

5. What are the top two ways that you can begin strengthening connections in your program?

   a.

   b.

6. What are the top two ways that you can begin communicating the positive impacts of your program?

   a.

   b.

A Final Word

Be an early educator who works with others to represent our voices in tune, our core knowledge base in its depth, our practices in their power, and our community in its glorious unity. Lead and engage. Keep an unblinking eye on the end goal. Pursue results. This final step in our 11-step journey to becoming architects of change grants us permission to celebrate—personally, collegially with our peers and colleagues, and publicly with the neighborhoods and communities where our beloved young children live and grow.

Overcoming Goliath

Let's Go!

> And there comes a time when one must take a position that is neither safe, nor politic, nor popular; but one must take it because it is right.
>
> —Dr. Martin Luther King Jr.[1]

We must take a fieldwide leadership position—because it is right. We cannot be intimidated, negated, or isolated anymore. You and I—ordinary people—can and must participate directly in creating positive social change for our children and for ourselves as a profession. We can defeat all of our Goliaths. We can do this, in the words of Martin Luther King, "to fulfill the American dream."[2]

As we close the pages on *The New Early Childhood Professional* and reflect on our conversation with you, our hearts are lifted by the raw and infinite potential in people who commit their lives to serve our young. Americans never hesitate to honor people who do good work. We celebrate those who serve in the military to preserve our deeply held democratic values. We give thanks for the physicians and nurses who lend care and relief when we ail or suffer. We champion the police, emergency caregivers, and first responders who shield us from harm. We cheer the dreamers who found a way to defy gravity—to fly, orbit the Earth, visit the moon, and open up the great frontier. And we applaud the thinkers who search for new ways to feed us, keep us warm, and cure our ills—or to simply understand the universe we call home.

To this list of heroes we add the women and men who teach and care for young children, those beautiful girls and boys who are our literal futures. Generations are nurtured in our family child-care homes, preschool centers, Head Start programs, and schools. Every child comes to us with enormous potential and unknown power. We have seen time and time again what one human being can achieve. And every child who comes through our door with a trusting smile and an open hand is pure and perfect and holds the potential of being a Mandela, a Parks, a Lincoln, an Esquival, a Bari, a Cortes, a Teresa, a Nhat Hanh, a Spielberg, a Walker (this glorious list could go on for pages). Some come to us bruised, or hurt, perhaps . . . too often underfed or underloved. We take them under our wing and open wide doors to the wonders of this life. We open those doors, keeping them safe while nudging them into their unknown futures.

There is no more breathtaking profession, no more magnificent calling.

We wrote *The New Early Childhood Professional* to remind you about who you are. Who we are. The respect we deserve, and the resources we must have. And now is the time that has come for us as we gather our courage, polish our stones, strengthen our ranks, and step into the fray to face the giants that limit our effectiveness.

An 11-step pathway to becoming architects of change has been presented. Each step is part of an integrated whole; the steps work together in a cycle as we face our realities (Step 1), acknowledge our strong knowledge base (Step 2), recognize any asymmetrical conflicts (Step 3), decide to face Goliath (Step 4), take stock of our own visions and identities as early educators (Step 5), identify a confidential community (step 6), explore our everyday challenges (Step 7), align what we know with what we do (Step 8), focus on what we want (Step 9), gather our allies (Step 10), and communicate our impact (Step 11).

Our fieldwide efforts to become architects of change matter deeply—for us and for those we serve. This four-path framework with 11 steps is intended to suggest the opportunity we have to seek equity and justice for our children and ourselves. We face Goliath because we recognize the possibilities of change (not fate), equality (not social hierarchy), and opportunity (not predestination). We face Goliath because we have hope.

We hope you come to think of this book as a companion, and that at least one step supports your journey when you are in need. Nothing would please us more than to know that your copy of the book had become dog-eared, worn from use, with yellow highlighting and turned-down corners—adapted to live in your situation. Use and debate the ideas among your colleagues. Use *The New Early Childhood Professional* to stimulate your thinking about professional development, for your personal growth or for activities with your team. The Five Smooth Stones, or activity ideas, throughout the book can be adapted for use in small-group or whole-staff workshops, training sessions, or planning meetings. We would love to hear about ways you've integrated the ideas of this book into your professional life.

And one final thought: Throughout the writing of this book, we've often asked ourselves, are we asking early educators not only to overcome Goliath, but to become Goliaths themselves—tall, proud, powerful—superior? We think not. Yes, we must work for the respect, resources, compensation, and influence we deserve. But the ideal we seek is that truly American ideal: What we really want is reconciliation and inclusion in a community of equals with other professions and with families.

We anticipate a journey, a marathon—not an event or a sprint. We have faith that, with dialogue and action, we can lead change for our profession and create conditions for change consistent with our knowledge base. We seek friendship and understanding with those who may see early care and education from perspectives different than our own. Our efforts are directed to unjust systems and inequalities, not toward individuals. We hope that early educators become a "beloved community," in the words of Dr. Martin Luther King Jr.[3] We know that this does not happen by chance—but by our willingness and strength to face Goliath.

> I come here tonight and plead with you:
> Believe in yourself and believe that you're somebody!
> . . . Nobody else can do this for us.
>
> —Dr. Martin Luther King Jr.[4]

Now is the time that has come for us as early educators. Let's go!

Please let us know what you think about The New Early Childhood Professional, *tell us your stories of challenge and success, and share the ways you've used this book in your work. Write to us at The CAYL Institute, Post Office Box 391378, Cambridge, Massachusetts 02139. Call us at 617-354-3820. Email info@cayl.org. And learn more about us at cayl.org.*

Notes

Introduction

1. King, 1968a.
2. Goffin & Washington, 2007.
3. All references to the story of David and Goliath are adapted from 1 Samuel 17:1–58, New International Version.
4. Dewey, 1938.
5. Kuhn, 1970.
6. Hegel, 1991.
7. Ames, 2010.
8. Offe, 1985.

Chapter 1

1. Arreguin-Toft, 2005.
2. Sherman & Hutton, 1989, p. 38.
3. Collins, 2001, p. 65.
4. Steiner, 1976.
5. Mann, 1848, p. 59.
6. Economist Intelligence Unit, 2012.
7. McLeigh, 2013.
8. Russell, 2014.
9. Marano, 2008.
10. Finkelhor, Turner, Ormrod, & Hamby, 2009.
11. The Center for the Prevention of Child Abuse, 2014.
12. Franke, 2014.
13. Children's Defense Fund, 2014.
14. Ibid.
15. Bassuk, DeCandia, Beach, & Berman, 2014.
16. Hart & Risley, 1995.
17. Feeding America, 2014.
18. Children's Defense Fund, 2014.
19. National Black Child Development Institute, 2013.
20. Spatig-Amerikaner, 2012.
21. National Conference of State Legislatures, 2014.

22. Derman-Sparks, LeeKeenan, & Nimmo, 2014.

23. For example, see Love, Chazan-Cohen, Raikes, & Brooks-Gunn, 2013.

24. For example, see Reardon, 2013.

25. Skinner, 2012.

26. Lascarides & Hinitz, 2013.

27. Haberman, 1988, p. 91.

28. Polanyi, 1958.

29. Colker, 2008, p. 68.

30. Duncan & Sojourner, 2013, pp. 945–968.

31. Polanyi, 1966.

32. Goffin, 2013; Goffin & Washington, 2007.

33. Palmer, 2007, p. 39.

34. Three of the most commonly cited studies used to indicate the power of early care and education are the Perry Preschool Project (Xiang, Barnett, Belfield & Nores, 2005), the Abecedarian Project (Barbarin et al., 2012), and the Chicago Child Parent Centers (Reynolds et al., 2011).

35. Palmer, 2007, p. 39.

36. Whitebook, Phillips, & Howes, 2014.

37. Ibid.

38. Ibid.

39. U.S. Census Bureau, 2010.

40. Barnett, Carolan, Squires, & Clarke Brown, 2013.

41. Obama, 2013.

42. Obama, 2015.

43. Goffin & Washington, 2007, p. 21.

44. Kagan & Kauerz, 2007, p. 21.

45. Miller & Almond, 2011.

46. Alliance for Early Childhood Finance, 2014.

47. Johnson, 1998.

48. Lorde, 2005, p. 90.

Chapter 2

1. Heffner, 2011.

2. Ellison, 1952, p. 3.

3. Jackson, 2014.

4. Barnett & Hustedt, 2011, p. 3.

5. Economist Intelligence Unit, 2012.

6. Schweich, 2013.

7. Washington, Marshall, Robinson, Modigliani, & Rosa, 2006.

8. Comer, 2009.

9. Putnam, 2000.

10. Palmer, 1983, p. 5.

11. Roth, 2004.

12. CAYL Institute, 2010–2014
13. Washington, 2008.
14. Maroto & Brandon, 2012.
15. Holm, Janairo, Jordan, & Wright, 2008.
16. Whitebook, Phillips, & Howes, 2014.
17. Ibid.
18. Ibid.
19. Rice, 2007.
20. Strauss, 2012.
21. Boser, 2011.
22. Mack, 1975.
23. Arreguin-Toft, 2005.
24. Lindbergh, 1991, p. 26.
25. Durant, 1957, p. 87
26. Weiner, 1980.
27. Adiele & Abraham, 2013.
28. McClelland, 1986.
29. King, 1968b.
30. King, 1965.
31. King, 1963a.
32. Kagan & Kauerz, 2012.

Chapter 3

1. Lewin, 1947.
2. Terkel, 2005.
3. The CAYL Institute's Core Principles:
   A. Representative Leadership: involving people in decisions that affect them.
   B. Commitment to Diversity: ensuring that all voices are heard and bridging multiple perspectives.
   C. Focused on Solutions: embracing responsibility to create sustainable change.
   D. Impact and Innovation: taking action that is timely, relevant, and immediately actionable.
   E. Building and Sharing Knowledge: creating and disseminating strategic information to be understood and used by everyone.
4. Washington, Marshall, Robinson, Modigliani, & Rosa, 2006.
5. Bowlby, 1982.
6. Ainsworth et al., 1978.
7. Fullan & Hargreaves, 2012.
8. Ibid.
9. Washington, B. T., 1895.
10. Ziglar, n.d.

11. Wilson, 2006.

12. GPU Nuclear Corporation, 1986. This quote's legitimacy is disputed.

13. Countdown to Kindergarten, 2009.

14. www.countdowntokindergarten.com/calendar/playcal.html

15. groundWork, 2006.

16. Paul & Elder, 2006.

17. Ruiz, 1997.

18. King, 1963b, p. 122.

19. Le Guin & Wood, 1979, p. 139.

20. Wong, 1999, p. 16.

21. Carter, 1996, p. 7.

22. Academy of Achievement, 1997.

23. Walker, 2011.

24. King, 1967.

25. Maxwell, 2007, p. 67.

26. Goodreads, 2014.

27. Taylor & McCloskey, 2008.

28. Rogers, n.d.

29. For more information on state-by-state requirements, please visit nrckids.org/index.cfm/resources/state-licensing-and-regulation-information/

30. Bodrova & Leong, 2007.

31. *Academic watch in Ohio*: school rates below expected growth for at least 3 consecutive years; *AYP*: Adequate Yearly Progress; *Rated excellent*: Increased AYP status, met 94–100% of indicators.

32. Kennedy, 1966.

33. Brandes, 2012.

34. Oregon Public Broadcasting, 2005 (updated reference).

35. Pascale, Sternin, & Sternin, 2010.

36. Ibid., p. 155.

37. Ibid., p. 138.

38. Lao-Tzu, 1963, p. 67.

39. Heifetz, 1994.

40. For example, see Heifetz, Grashow, & Linsky, 2009.

41. Ibid.

42. Senge, Kleiner, Roberts, Ross, Roth, & Smith, 1999, p. 16.

43. Senge, 2008.

44. Kahane, 2010.

45. Searle, 2012.

46. Williamson, 1992, p. 190.

Chapter 4

1. Peters, 2011.

2. McCarthy & Zald, 2001.

3. Twain, 1889, p. 422.

4. Harrison, 1988.

5. Rauzi, 2013.

6. Hunter, J., n.d.

7. Smith, 1790, p. 43.

8. Washington & Hagan, 2009.

9. Holm, Janairo, Jordan, & Wright, 2008.

10. Covey, 1989.

11. Goldman & Papson, 1998, p. 49.

12. *The Vedas* are a collection of hymns and other religious texts composed in India between about 1500 and 1000 BCE. See Hanlon, 2012, p. 128.

13. Committee for Economic Development, 2012.

14. Kanter, 2004.

15. Caroselli, 2000, p. 71.

16. Nash, 1997.

17. Guernsey, Bornfreund, McCann, & Williams, 2014.

18. Ibid.

19. Nall Bales, 2010.

20. Gienapp, Reisman, Langley, Cohen, Cipollone, Kelly, Crary, & Lin, 2010.

21. Brown, 2011.

22. Strategic Research Group, 2010.

Conclusion

1. King, 1968b.

2. King, 1964.

3. King, 1957.

4. Mrholtshistory, 2008.

References

Academy of Achievement. (1997, January 22). Maya Angelou interview: America's Renaissance woman. Available at www.achievement.org/autodoc/page/ang0int-1

Adiele, E. E., & Abraham, N. (2013). Achievement of Abraham Maslow's needs hierarchy theory among teachers: Implications for human resource management in the secondary school system in Rivers State. *Journal of Curriculum and Teaching, 2*(1), 140.

Ainsworth, M. D. S., Blehar, M. C., Waters, E., & Wall, S. (1978). *Patterns of attachment: A psychological study of the strange situation.* Mahwah, NJ: Lawrence Erlbaum Associates.

Alliance for Early Childhood Finance. (2014). Finance. Washington, DC: Author. Available at www.earlychildhoodfinance.org/finance

Ames, R., & Hall, D. (2010). *Dao de jing: A philosophical translation.* New York, NY: Random House.

Arreguin-Toft, I. (2005). *How the weak win wars: A theory of asymmetric conflict.* New York, NY: Cambridge University Press.

Barbarin, O. A., Burchinal, M., Campbell, F. A., Kainz, K., Pan, Y., Pungello, E. P., Sparling, J. J., Ramey, C. T., & Wasik, B. H. (2012, July). Adult outcomes as a function of an early childhood educational program: An Abecedarian Project follow-up. *Developmental Psychology, 48*(4), 1033–1043. DOI: 10.1037/a0026644

Barnett, W. S., Carolan, M. E., Squires, J. H., & Clarke Brown, K. (2013). *The state of preschool 2013: State preschool yearbook.* New Brunswick, NJ: National Institute for Early Education Research.

Barnett, W. S., & Hustedt, J. T. (2011, April). Improving public financing for early learning programs. [Policy brief 23]. New Brunswick, NJ: National Institute for Early Education Research.

Bassuk, E. L., DeCandia, C. J., Beach, C. A., & Berman, F. (2014). *America's youngest outcasts: A report card on child homelessness.* Waltham, MA: National Center on Family Homelessness.

Bodrova, E., & Leong. D.J. (2007). *Tools of the mind*: The Vygotskian approach to *early childhood education* (2nd ed.). Columbus, OH: Merrill/Prentice Hall.

Boser, U. (2011, November). Teacher diversity matters: A state-by-state analysis of teachers of color. Washington, DC: The Center for American

Progress. Available at www.americanprogress.org/wp-content/uploads/issues/2011/11/pdf/teacher_diversity.pdf

Bowlby, J. (1982). *Attachment: Attachment and loss Vol. 1.* London, England: The Hogarth Press.

Brandes, P. (2012, July 20). Want to bridge? DISRUPT! *Social Capital Blog.* In association with Saguaro Seminar: Civic Engagement in America. Available at socialcapital.wordpress.com/2012/07/20/guest-post-want-to-bridge-disrupt/

Brown, J. (2011, Augusts 16). Brian Tracy: Reinventing yourself for success. Addicted2Success [video]. Available at addicted2success.com/success-advice/video-brian-tracy-re-inventing-yourself-for-success/

Caroselli, M. (2000). *Leadership skills for managers.* New York, NY: McGraw-Hill.

Carter, S. L. (1996). *Integrity.* New York, NY: Basic Books.

CAYL Institute. (2010–2014). *Conversations with early educators.* Boston, MA: Author.

The Center for the Prevention of Child Abuse. (2014). *Child abuse fact sheet.* The Center for the Prevention of Child Abuse of Dutchess County. Available at www.preventchildabusedutchess.org/statistics

Children's Defense Fund. (2014). *The state of America's children® 2014 report.* Washington, DC: Author.

Colker, L. J. (2008, March). Twelve characteristics of effective early childhood teachers. *Young Children, 63*(2), 68.

Collins, J. C. (2001). *Good to great: Why some companies make the leap—and others don't.* New York, NY: HarperBusiness.

Comer, J. P. (2009). *What I learned in school: Reflections on race, child development, and school reform.* San Francisco: Jossey-Bass.

Committee for Economic Development. (2012, June 26). *Unfinished business: Continued investment in child care and early learning is critical to business and America's future.* Washington, DC: Author. Available at www.ced.org/reports/single/unfinished-business

Countdown to Kindergarten. (2009). Welcome. Available at www.countdowntokindergarten.com/

Covey, S. R. (1989). *The seven habits of highly effective people: Wisdom and insight from* (Mini. ed.). Philadelphia, PA: Running Press.

Derman-Sparks, L., LeeKeenan, D., & Nimmo, J. (2014). *Leading anti-bias early childhood programs: A guide for change.* New York, NY: Teachers College Press.

Dewey, J. (1938). *Experience and education.* New York, NY: Macmillan.

Duncan, G. J., & Sojourner, A. J. (Fall 2013). Can intensive early childhood intervention programs eliminate income-based cognitive and achievement gaps? *Journal of Human Resources, 48*(4), 945–968.

Durant, W. (1957). *The story of philosophy; The lives and opinions of the greater philosophers from Plato to John Dewey.* New York, NY: Pocket Books.

Economist Intelligence Unit. (2012). Starting well: Benchmarking early education across the world. *The Economist Intelligence Unit Limited*. New York, NY. A report commissioned by the Lien Foundation: Singapore.

Ellison, R. (1952). *Invisible man*. Franklin Center, PA: Franklin Library.

Feeding America. (2014). Impact of hunger. Available at feedingamerica.org/hunger-in-america/impact-of-hunger.aspx

Finkelhor, D., Turner, H., Ormrod, R., & Hamby, S. L. (2009, October 5). Violence, abuse, and crime exposure in a national sample of children and youth. *Pediatrics, 124*(5), 1411–1423.

Franke, H. A. (2014). Toxic stress: Effects, prevention and treatment. *Children, 1*(3), 390–402.

Fullan, M., & Hargreaves, A. (2012, June 6) Reviving teaching with "professional capital." *Education Week Magazine*. Available at edweek.org/ew/articles/2012/06/06/33hargreaves_ep.h31.html30-36

Gienapp, A., Reisman, J., Langley, K., Cohen, C., Cipollone, T., Kelly, T., Crary, D., & Lin Chong, S. (2010). Strategic communications for influence: Lessons from the Annie E. Casey Foundation and its KIDS COUNT initiative. *The Foundation Review, 1*(4) 14–27.

Goffin, S. (2013). *Early childhood education for a new era*. New York, NY: Teachers College Press.

Goffin, S., & Washington, V. (2007). *Ready or not*. New York, NY: Teachers College Press.

Goldman, R., & Papson, S. (1998). *Nike culture: The sign of the swoosh*. London, England: Sage Publications.

Goodreads. (2014). William G. T. Shedd. Available at goodreads.com/quotes/1388-a-ship-is-safe-in-harbor-but-that-s-not-what

GPU Nuclear Corporation. (1986, June). *Black Enterprise, 16*(11), 79.

groundWork. (2006). Full-day kindergarten: Expanding learning opportunities. Available at groundworkohio.org/resources/policybrief_pdf/020109%20Full-Day%20Kindergarten%20Expanding%20Learning%20Opportunities.pdf

Guernsey, L., Bornfreund, L., McCann, C., & Williams, C. (2014, January). Subprime learning: Early Education in America since the Great Recession. New America: Education Policy Program. Available at newamerica.net/sites/newamerica.net/files/policydocs/NewAmerica_SubprimeLearning_Release.pdf

Haberman, M. (1988). Gatekeepers to the profession. In B. Spodek, O. N. Saracho, & D. L. Peters (Eds.), *Professionalism and the early childhood practitioner* (pp. 84–92). New York, NY: Teachers College Press.

Hanlon, B. (2012). *The change your life book*. Deerfield Beach, FL: Health Communications.

Harrison, G. (1988). Any road. *Brainwashed*. Parlophone, Dark Horse.

Hart, B., & Risley, T. R. (1995). The early catastrophe. The 30 million word gap by age 3. *Meaningful differences in the everyday experiences of young American children.* Available at www.gsa.gov/graphics/pbs/The_Early_Catastrophe_30_Million_Word_Gap_by_Age_3.pdf

Heffner, C. L. (2011). *Personality synopsis.* AllPsych Online. Available at www.allpsych.com/personalitysynopsis/index html

Hegel, G. W. F. (1991). *Hegel: Elements of the philosophy of right.* London, England: Cambridge University Press.

Heifetz, R. (1994). *Leadership without easy answers.* Cambridge, MA: Belknap Press of Harvard University Press.

Heifetz, R., Grashow, A., & Linsky, M. (2009). The theory behind the practice. *The practice of adaptive leadership* (p. 19). Boston, MA: Harvard Business Press.

Holm, J., Janairo, R., Jordan, T., & Wright, N. (2008). *Where are the men? Promoting gender diversity in the Massachusetts early childhood workforce.* Cambridge, MA: The CAYL Schott Fellowship in Early Care and Education. Available at cayl.org/wp-content/uploads/2013/05/Men.pdf

Hunter, J. (n.d.). Getting real about mindfulness. Jeremyhunter.net. Available at jeremyhunter.net/2013/07/getting-real-about-mcmindfulness/

Jackson, E. (2014, May 23). Sun Tzu's 31 best pieces of leadership advice. *Forbes Magazine.* Available at www.forbes.com/sites/ericjackson/2014/05/23/sun-tzus-33-best-pieces-of-leadership-advice/

Johnson, S. (1998). *Who moved my cheese?: An amazing way to deal with change in your work and in your life.* New York, NY: Putnam.

Kagan, S. L., & Kauerz, K. (2007). Reaching for the whole: Integration and alignment in early education policy. In R. C. Pianta, M. J. Cox, & K. L. Snow (Eds.), *School readiness and the transition to kindergarten in the era of accountability* (pp. 3–30). Baltimore, MD: Paul H. Brookes Publishing.

Kagan, S. L., & Kauerz, K. (2012). *Early childhood systems: Transforming early learning.* New York, NY: Teachers College.

Kahane, A. (2010). *Power and love: A theory and practice of social change.* San Francisco, CA: Berrett-Koehler Publications.

Kanter, R. E. (2004). *Confidence: How winning streaks and losing streaks begin and end.* New York, NY: Three Rivers Press.

Kennedy, R. F. (1966, June 6). "Day of affirmation" [speech]. University of Cape Town, Cape Town, South Africa. Available at rfksafilm.org/html/speeches/unicape.php

King, Jr., M. L. (1957, April 7). "The birth of a nation" [speech presented at Dexter Avenue Baptist Church in Montgomery, AL]. Available at mlk-kpp01.stanford.edu/index.php/kingpapers/article/the_birth_of_a_new_nation_sermon_delivered_at_dexter_avenue_baptist_church/

King, Jr., M. L. (1963a, April 16). Letter from Birmingham Jail. Reprinted in J. Williams (1988), *Eyes on the prize* (p. 187). New York, NY: Penguin.

King, Jr., M. L. (1963b). *Strength to love.* New York, NY: Harper & Row.

King, Jr., M. L. (1964, February 5). "The American dream" [speech presented at Drew University in Madison, NJ]. Available at mlk-kpp01.stanford.edu/index.php/encyclopedia/documentsentry/doc_the_american_dream/

King, Jr., M. L. (1965, June). Remaining awake through a great revolution [speech]. Commencement Address for Oberlin College, Oberlin, OH.

King, Jr., M. L. (1967, August 16). Where do we go from here? Annual report delivered at the 11th Convention of the Southern Christian Leadership Conference, Atlanta, GA.

King, Jr., M. L. (1968a, February 6). "A proper sense of priorities" [speech presented to Clergy and Laymen Concerned about Vietnam, Washington, DC]. Available at www.aavw.org/special_features/speeches_speech_king04.html

King, Jr., M. L. (1968b, March 31). "Remaining awake through a great revolution" [speech delivered at the National Cathedral in Washington, DC]. Available at mlk-kpp01.stanford.edu/index.php/encyclopedia/multimediaentry/doc_remaining_awake_through_a_great_revolution/

Kuhn, T. S. (1970). *The structure of scientific revolutions.* Chicago, IL: University of Chicago Press.

Lao-Tzu. (1963). *Tao te ching* (D. C. Lau, Ed.). London: Penguin.

Lascarides, V. C., & Hinitz, B. F. (2013). *History of early childhood education* (Vol. 982). London, England: Routledge.

Le Guin, U. K., & Wood, S. (1979). *The language of the night: Essays on fantasy and science fiction.* New York, NY: Putnam.

Lewin, K. (1947, June). Frontiers in group dynamics: Concept, method and reality in social science; Social equilibria and social change. *Human Relations, 1*(1), 34–35,

Lindbergh, A. M. (1991). *Gift from the sea.* New York, NY: Vintage.

Lorde, A. (2005). *Conversations with Audre Lorde.* Jackson, MS: University Press of Mississippi.

Love, J. M., Chazan-Cohen, R., Raikes, H., & Brooks-Gunn, J. (2013, February). What makes a difference: Early Head Start evaluation findings in a developmental context [Monograph]. *Society for Research in Child Development, 78*(1), vii–viii, 1–173. DOI: 10.1111/j.1540-5834.2012.00699.x

Mack, J. R. (1975, January). Why big nations lose small wars: The politics of asymmetric conflicts. *World Politics, 27*(2), 175–200.

Mann, H. (1848). *Twelfth annual report of the board of education, together with the twelfth annual report of the secretary of the board.* Boston, MA: Dutton and Wentworth.

Marano, H. E. (2008). *A nation of wimps: The high cost of invasive parenting.* New York, NY: Broadway.

Maroto, M. L., & Brandon, R. N. (2012). Summary of background data on the ECCE workforce. In Institute of Medicine & National Research Council

(Eds.), *The early childhood care and education workforce: Challenges and opportunities* [workshop report]. Washington, DC: The National Academies Press.

Maxwell, J. C. (2007). *The Maxwell daily reader: 365 days of insight to develop the leader within you and influence those around you.* Nashville, TN: Thomas Nelson.

McCarthy, J. D., & Zald, M. N. (2001). The enduring vitality of the resource mobilization theory of social movements. In J. H. Turner & M. N. Zald (Ed.), *Handbook of sociological theory* (pp. 533–565). New York, NY: Kluwer Academic/Plenum.

McClelland, D. C. (1986). Some reflections on the two psychologies of love. *Journal of Personality, 54*(2), 334–353.

McLeigh, J. D. (2013). How to form alliances with families and communities: The provision of informal supports to families keeps kids safe. *Child Abuse & Neglect, 37,* 17–28.

Miller, E., & Almond, J. (2011, November). *The crisis in early education: A research-based case for more play and less pressure.* New York, NY: Alliance for Childhood.

Mrholtshistory. (2008, April 20). *Martin Luther King Jr.—I'm black and I'm beautiful* [video file]. Available at www.youtube.com/watch?v=nGLF0X3WIiE

Nall Bales, S. (2010). *Framing education reform: A FrameWorks message memo.* Washington, DC: FrameWorks Institute.

Nash, J. M. (1997, February 3). How a child's brain develops and what it means for child care and welfare reform. *Time, 149*(5), 48–63.

National Black Child Development Institute. (2013). *Being black is not a risk factor.* Washington, DC: Author.

National Conference of State Legislatures. (2014, April). Allow in-state tuition for undocumented students. Denver, CO & Washington, DC: National Conference of State Legislatures. Available at www.ncsl.org/research/education/undocumented-student-tuition-state-action.aspx

Obama, B. (2013, February 12). State of the Union Address. Available at www.whitehouse.gov/state-of-the-union-2013

Obama, B. (2015, January 20). State of the Union Address. Available at www.whitehouse.gov/sotu

Offe, C. (1985). New social movements: Challenging the boundaries of institutional politics. *Social Research, 52*(4), 817–868.

Oregon Public Broadcasting. (2005). What is social entrepreneurship? *The New Heroes.* Oregon Public Broadcasting and Malone-Grove Productions Inc. Available at pbs.org/opb/thenewheroes/whatis/p_index.html

Palmer, P. (1983). *To know as we are known: A spirituality of education.* San Francisco, CA: Harper & Row.

Palmer, P. J. (2007). *The courage to teach: Exploring the inner landscape of a teacher's life* (10th Anniversary Ed.). San Francisco, CA: Jossey-Bass.

Pascale, R. T., Sternin, J., & Sternin, M. (2010). *The power of positive deviance: How unlikely innovators solve the world's problems.* Cambridge, MA: Harvard University Press.

Paul, R., & Elder, L. (2006). *Critical thinking: Learn the tools the best thinkers use.* (Concise Ed.). Upper Saddle River, NJ: Prentice Hall.

Peters, T. (2011, December 5). Excellence now: Action [E-reader version]. Available at itunes.apple.com/us/book/excellence-now-action/id486659252?mt=11

Polanyi, M. (1958). *Personal knowledge: Towards a post-critical philosophy.* Chicago, IL: University of Chicago Press.

Polanyi, M. (1966). *The tacit dimension.* Chicago, IL: University of Chicago Press.

Putnam, R. D. (2000). *Bowling alone: The collapse and revival of American community.* New York, NY: Simon & Schuster.

Rauzi, R. (2013, February 23). Tapping into the power of mindfulness. *The Los Angeles Times.* Available at articles.latimes.com/2013/feb/23/business/la-fi-meditation-management-20130224

Reardon, S. F. (2013). The widening income achievement gap. *Educational Leadership, 70*(8), 10–16.

Reynolds, A. J., Temple, J. A., White, B. A., Ou, S. R., & Robertson, D. L. (2011). Age 26 cost–benefit analysis of the child-parent center early education program. *Child Development, 82*(1), 379–404.

Rhodes, H., & Huston, A. (2012). Building the workforce our children deserve. Sharing child and youth development knowledge. *Social Policy Report, 26,* 1, 3–26.

Rice, C. (2007, January). *Building strong rungs to build sturdy ladders* [policy brief]. Newark, NJ: Association for Children of New Jersey. Available at acnj.org/admin.asp?uri=2081&action=15&di=970&ext=pdf&view=yes

Rogers, W. (n.d.). Will Rogers. *OMPage.* Available at ompage.net/Text/Will_Rogers.htm

Roth, S. A. (2004). *Family child care providers' self-reported perceptions of isolation, autonomy and burnout* [doctoral dissertation]. Available at Electronic Doctoral Dissertations for UMass Amherst. (Paper AAI3136774)

Rowling, J. K. (2001). *Harry Potter and the sorcerer's stone.* New York, NY: Scholastic.

Ruiz, M. (1997). T*he four agreements: A practical guide to personal freedom.* San Rafael, CA: Amber-Allen Publications.

Russell, M. H. (2014). Connecting children to nature in a Montessori primary environment (Doctoral dissertation, University of Wisconsin–River Falls). Available at minds.wisconsin/edu/handle/1793/69013

1 Samuel 17: 1–58, New International Version.

Schweich, T. A. (2013, June). Early childhood development, education, and care fund [Report No. 2013–046]. Available at auditor.mo.gov/Press/2013-046.pdf

Searle, R. (2012, March 2). Seven sources of leadership power. *The Business Spectator.* Available at businessspectator.com.au/article/2012/3/2/resources-and-energy/seven-sources-leadership-power

Senge, P. M. (2008). *The necessary revolution: Working together to create a sustainable world.* New York, NY: Broadway Books.

Senge, P., Kleiner, A., Roberts, C., Ross, R., Roth, G., & Smith, B. (1999). *The dance of change.* London, England: Nicholas Brealey.

Sherman, S.P., & Hutton, C. (1989, March 27). Inside the mind of Jack Welch. *Fortune Magazine, 119*(7), 38.

Skinner, C. (April, 2012). *Protecting the safety net in tough times: Lessons from the states.* New York, NY: National Center for Children in Poverty, Mailman School of Public Health, Columbia University.

Smith, A. (1790). *The theory of moral sentiments.* London: A. Millar.

Snow, K. (2013, November 13). *Who is the early care and education workforce?* Washington, DC: National Association for the Education of Young Children. Available at www.naeyc.org/blogs/gclarke/2013/11/who-early-care-and-education-workforce-0

Spatig-Amerikaner, A. (2012, August). *Unequal education: Federal loophole enables lower spending on students of color.* Washington, DC: Center for American Progress. Available at www.americanprogress.org/wp-content/uploads/2012/08/UnequalEduation.pdf

Steiner, G. Y. (1976). *The children's cause.* Washington, DC: Brookings Institution.

Strategic Research Group. (2010, October). *Assessing the effectiveness of Tennessee's pre-kindergarten program: Second annual report.* Nashville, TN: Tennessee Comptroller of the Treasury.

Strauss, V. (2012, February 7). Texas schools chief calls testing obsession a "perversion." *The Washington Post.* Available at www.washingtonpost.com/blogs/answer-sheet/post/texas-schools-chief-calls-testing-obsession-a-perversion/02/05/gIQA5FUWvQ_blog.html

Taylor, D., & McCloskey, M. (2008, June 6). How to pick a president. *Christianity Today.* Available at christianitytoday.com/ct/2008/june/17.22.html

Terkel, S. (2005, October 24). Community in action. Special series: This I believe. National Public Radio. Available at npr.org/templates/story/story.php?storyId=4963443

Twain, M. (1889). *A Connecticut yankee in King Arthur's court.* New York, NY and London, England: Harper & Brothers Publishers.

U.S. Bureau of Labor Statistics. (2014a, January 8). Kindergarten and elementary school teachers. *Occupational Outlook Handbook 2014–15 Edition.* Washington, DC: U.S. Department of Labor, Available at www.bls.gov/ooh/education-training-and-library/kindergarten-and-elementary-school-teachers.htm

U.S. Bureau of Labor Statistics. (2014b, January 8). Preschool and childcare directors. *Occupational Outlook Handbook 2014–15 Edition.* Washington, DC:

U.S. Department of Labor. Available at www.bls.gov/ooh/management/preschool-and-childcare-center-directors.htm

U.S. Bureau of Labor Statistics. (2014c, January 8). Preschool teachers. *Occupational Outlook Handbook 2014–15 Edition.* Washington, DC: U.S. Department of Labor. Available at www.bls.gov/ooh/education-training-and-library/preschool-teachers.htm

U.S. Census Bureau. (2010). The education path of our nation. Washington: DC: Author. Available at www.census.gov/how/infographics/education.html

Walker, R. (2011, December 12). An interview with Ericka Huggins: The fire this time. Ella Baker Center for Human Rights. Available at ellabakercenter.org/blog/2011/12/an-interview-with-ericka-huggins-the-fire-this-time

Washington, B. T. (1895, September 18). Atlanta compromise [speech]. Available at historymatters.gmu.edu/d/39

Washington, V. (2007). *Persistent disparities: The impact of race and class on young children and what Michigan can do about it.* Cambridge, MA: The Schott Fellowship in Early Care and Education. Available at od.msue.msu.edu/uploads/files/...Diversity/Persistant_Disparities.pdf

Washington, V. (2008). *Role, relevance, reinvention: Higher education in the field of early care and education.* Boston, MA: Wheelock College.

Washington, V., & Hagan, W. (2009, July). *FIRST, DO NO HARM!* Cambridge, MA: The CAYL Institute. Available at cayl.org/wp-content/uploads/2013/05/FINAL-Assessment-Policy-Paper.pdf

Washington, V., Marshall, N., Robinson, C., Modigliani, K., & Rosa, M. (2006, February 14). *Keeping the promise: A study of the Massachusetts child care voucher system.* Boston, MA: The Bessie Tartt Wilson Initiative for Children.

Weiner, B. (1980). *Human motivation.* New York, NY: Holt, Rinehart and Winston.

Whitebook, M., Phillips, D., & Howes, C. (2014). *Worthy work, STILL unlivable wages: The early childhood workforce 25 years after the national child care staffing study.* Center for the Study of Child Care Employment Institute for Research on Labor and Employment, University of California, Berkeley.

Williamson, M. (1992). *A return to love: Reflections on the principles of a course in miracles.* New York, NY: HarperCollins.

Wilson, J. (2006). Solid rocket boosters. National Aeronautics and Space Administration. Available at www.nasa.gov/returntoflight/system/system_SRB.html

Wong, B. (Ed.). (1999). *Quotations for the wayside.* Boston, MA: Unitarian Universalist Association.

Xiang, A., Barnett, W. S., Belfield, C. R., & Nores, M. (2005). *Lifetime effects: The High/Scope Perry Preschool Study through age 40.* Ypsilanti, MI: High/Scope Press.

Ziglar. (n.d.). Official Ziglar quotes. Available at www.ziglar.com/quotes/you-dont-have-be-great-start

Index

About the Authors

Dr. Valora Washington is the chief executive officer of the Council for Professional Recognition and the founder of the CAYL Institute. She has served on numerous federal, state, and local boards or commissions and coauthored over 50 publications. She is a certified association executive with the American Society of Association Executives™.

Brenda Gadson is owner/operator of BMG Consulting. She specializes in working with community-based nonprofits, providing a variety of activities designed to support, sustain, and strengthen them. She holds an MPA from Clark University and an undergraduate degree from Tufts University. Married for 41 years, she is a mother of two children and grandmother of one, Kennedi Virginia.

Kathryn L. Amel, a graduate of Boston University, has been with CAYL for the past 4 years. Kathryn is proficient in the co-creation, development, and implementation of high-quality events, networking meetings, and technical assistance opportunities for early educators. She is passionate about children, animals, and the environment, and enjoys yoga, rollerblading, and tea.